Delusion of Mind

Strength Through Spirit

A journey from the Light into
darkness and a return to the Light

Robert Ernest Bach

ISBN-10: 1542583683

ISBN-13: 978-1542583688

Cover Photo
by
Scott Indermaur
www.indermaurmedia.com

Cover Design
by
Kyle Blackmar
KJB Creative

RE Bach
187 Main Street
East Greenwich, RI 02818
RobertErnestBach.com

DEDICATION

With love and appreciation to my wife Mia
and children, Madison, Demetria, and Hans
To you the reader and journeyer,
and to the Most High,
The Grand Architect

CONTENTS

ACKNOWLEDGMENTS

To the countless men and women who have been a part of my journey and who have allowed me to be a part of their journey, past, present, and future.

To my wife Mia who has always stood at my side with a spirit of patience, love, tolerance and kindliness like no other. Your belief in me and tireless efforts are an inspiration.

PREFACE

My name is Bobby and I'm an alcoholic. I didn't set out to be an alcoholic, or did I?

Actually I'm a recovered alcoholic. I've been sober for just over thirty years now and enjoy a life beyond my wildest dreams, though it wasn't always so. I'm happily married with three beautiful children. My children are grown now and my wife and I only have one still at home.

What makes me a "recovered" alcoholic? The fast and short answer is that I was able to get reconnected to God. And my hope is that within these pages I will be able to explain this in more depth. But before I can get there, to my present space in heart, soul and mind, I must go back. Way back to the beginning of it all.

At the outset of my drinking, and other vices picked up along the way, there were always underlying reasons, causes, that propelled me to a life of self-destruction. This is where my story must begin, hopefully giving you a clear picture and idea of how one can become so ill in spirit and mind.

Before we become intimately involved with one

another I feel it's important to let you know at the outset of this writing a few things to understand about me. First things first, I'm not a writer. I did not graduate high school, I was too high to do that. So I ask you for patience as you make your way through these pages. I may use some words over and over and will undoubtedly repeat some information. The repeating of information may be intentional at times to make a point. I will share with you some really personal details about my life. Some of these my own family may not know anything about. I do not have relationships with my family in that traditional idea of family and perhaps some of these family members are here with you.

Which leads me to my next point before we take a trip back in time. My intent for writing.

I have made absolute, yes full, peace with my past and all that was, and is, back there. I hold no one person, family or friend, in contempt for their own position in my life, past or present. I am not writing from a place of malice, anger or hate. I'm writing from a place of love. If you are a family member, or friend, and you come up in these pages know that all that is written here is based on my own experience, strength and hope which was mutually shared by and between us. I had a therapist that once said to me "Each time you begin a statement with 'I think, I feel or I believe' it is authentically yours as your own experience. Not one person can argue with what is authentically yours."

The only argument I can make with what Peter said to me as I sat with him during a painful session a few months after my first child was born, questioning "How the hell am I supposed to be a parent?," is this.

Each statement that begins with one of those identifiers is based on one's own perceptions by what was taught to them. What ideas, emotions, and attitudes that were derived out of those teachings ultimately setting up guiding forces that determine one's decisions.

This is why we must start from the beginning. An effort to go back in time to fully examine with you, in an open manner, how the *guiding forces* were set up in my life, right from the start, that brought me to begin drinking at the early age of 12. And then a look at how in just six short years I was forced to leave high school two weeks before my graduation as I just couldn't go on any further. Landing me in a rehab for 30 days that would begin to shift the direction in my life to the here and now.

The bottom line is that I experienced a separation from God, a God that I now know was innately installed in me. I tried with every ounce of my own *self-will* to live life and it all ended in a severe failure, then a renewed relationship with my Creator.

I believe we all have an *idea* of God. That we are each born with it. I believe it either gets nurtured or is brutally removed from us through the circumstances in our lives. I further believe that whichever the case may be for you it is truly the way it was supposed to be for you and that we each have a path and purpose that needs to be fulfilled. If the idea of God sickens you or makes you uncomfortable, I get it. I really get it! The idea at one time would make me ill. And that would drive me further away from Him.

In an effort to make the writing smoother and without some sort of fanciness to try and rope you in by substituting different labels for God such as

Creator, Sunlight Of The Spirit, Spirit, Nature, Grand Architect or whatever makes it palatable for you I will go with just plain "God" as I type. If I deviate and become forgetful I'll be sure to give Him a big letter at the front of His Name.

Our circumstances and experiences may not be the same yet perhaps you will relate to some of what I have experienced, or more pointedly to how those guiding forces were set up in your own life. I wish you peace and love as you read and maybe even a bit of uncomfortability if it is meant to be that way for you.

I will start at the beginning and try my hardest to keep it all in line. Yet on occasion I will deviate. When this happens I'll clearly define when by mixing in chapters titled "Intermezzo," a break in the drama.

It would be wise to touch on that *perspective* a bit to give you a clearer point to ponder, or perhaps to share with you where this writing is coming from. I shared that I am clean and sober and have been for over thirty years. I got sober at the age of eighteen just two weeks shy of graduating high school. I had the fortune of two choices when I hit that bottom as a crack appeared in my shell and *mask*. Truth was allowed into me and it was at this point that I admitted complete defeat, with regard to the drinking and drugging. I had two choices. A stay on the grounds of what we grew up knowing then as the IMH. The Institute of Mental Health, also known as the prison grounds within Rhode Island. The other choice, afforded to me only because my father had great health insurance and at the time these plans covered a thirty day stay in a rehab, was a country club treatment facility. Given the choice I went with the logical, human-inspired easier road. I chose the rehab. Besides I knew something about this place which I will share about later as we journey.

As a consequence of that mini vacation from life I was exposed to many others who were also clean and sober. And their chief method of gaining recovery and staying sober was through a program called Alcoholics Anonymous. This book is not entirely about that particular program or fellowship yet my perspective today was reached through it, the people who are members of it, and more importantly the actual *program*. The program being its twelve steps. A miraculous set of principles if one has the actual balls to fully follow.

I will not get into the details of my journey through the work at this point but I thought it wise to let you know that it was my experience through them that allowed me to gain freedom and release from all of those things that can bind us to that destructive self, ego.

This book is not solely about Alcoholics Anonymous, that is for another time and place. It is about a journey that I believe each of us begins when we are shot onto this scene in our meatsuits, our physical bodies. It's about a journey home to God.

If you are in one of the many recovery programs out there you might be able to identify with my journey. If you are having difficulties with a vice you may be inspired to look at these principles as a means to gain freedom from them. I have seen many fully recover. And regretfully I have seen so many fail and fall by the wayside. I will reference parts of the actual twelve steps and even some of what the pioneers of those principles came upon and left to us in their writings, and experience. This I will have to do as my own experience has come to match theirs, and their own discoveries. A near identical match to what they left us in their book *Alcoholics Anonymous,* the first part of the book that contains what they referred to as the *program.*

I've wanted to write all of this so many times and have often wondered if I could do it.

I have recently left Alcoholics Anonymous "meetings," not the principles. How did this happen? I'll get into that part later on as well. It was my departure that brought about this writing. I was hesitant to begin and didn't know where to start. My family's recent move into a new home has brought about many changes, as you can imagine. Once settled in and as my distance from the meetings grew I kept hearing this one word. "Write." It began as a whisper. A small sign. An intuitive nudge if you will. An omen.

I tried to ignore it. I felt as though I've tried three times and it always ended in failure, so why bother. The more I tried to ignore it the louder the whisper became. I would wake at crazy hours throughout the night. I find God does this to me at times so we might speak with one another. Myself through verbal grumbling with a background of impatience. And He through those intuitive nudges. The more I would ignore that "write," the louder or more severe the middle of the night wake up calls.

A couple of weeks ago a client stopped into the flower shop for a small gift. I hadn't seen her in a while and I know a bit about her "story." We all have a "story." As we spoke and shared with one another she spoke about a book she wrote and published and that she was doing a book signing. This on top of those intuitive nudges. I didn't have the courage to ask questions about my own thoughts or pushes to write. I settled on questions about her writing and experience. I ignored that *nudge*. Just another day at work, right?

This past week I was called to wake up in the middle of the night yet again. Violently. Like I was thrown out of the bed awakened. This really pissed me off! All I could think of was the day ahead, of an installation for a holiday party in Providence. I'm a floral and event designer and always work best under pressure but not without rest. I came downstairs and settled on the fact that I was not going to drift back off to sleep, made a cup of coffee and *watched* the anger within. As I sat in a chair and accepted that there was a reason God woke me up I thought to put Netflix on and a movie that could serve as background noise as I waited for those *messages* to reveal themselves.

All that came to me was..."Write."

All I could do was ask "How?" What came to be this day was pretty amazing, especially if you look for signs.

My friend Donna appeared in the design space again "looking for a gift." As she and my wife spoke about her book and her signing the courage appeared to ask some questions left unanswered from her previous visit. Her five minute visit turned into an hour of sharing back and forth and I was able to reveal my thoughts and concerns. And the ambivalence I was experiencing. I was able to skip leaning on Google for an answer as to "How."

As I shared more and more and finally asked

"how" she answered without hesitation. She simply said that all I spoke to actually contained two books and that she felt as though I was trying to mash them together. She offered that this is what was creating the confusion and hesitation. This coming to understand the hesitation opened the flow within. Another perspective came into view and a choice had to be made. Which one do I write first? Obviously we will see the answer together.

Lastly, this manuscript was in the hands of nine different people of varying backgrounds and stations in life before being published. It was an effort to gauge different responses. Their own positions in their journeys through life as humans has no relevance to you yet I believe their reactions may. It is their reaction that might serve as a prelude to your own. There will be times when you will absolutely relate to my journey though the circumstances between you and I may be different. And with this relation you may be brought to tears or the extreme opposite, laughter. At times you may be shocked. I'm confident there will be times you may wish to throw the writing across the room as I have wanted to when I went back to edit. I'm equally confident that there may be times when you might beg for five more minutes of time to continue the journey with me. These were a few of the reactions from those who favored me with their time, patience, and trust.

Each of them were brutally honest with me as this was exactly what I asked of them. I wished to know if there was value in the story for them. This is now up to you as well.

As this is the first title I've written I ask only one thing of you as we begin. Please extend me your patience.

Strap yourself in, fasten your seatbelt, try to keep your hands and feet in the vehicle when it gets rough and let them fly free when triumph is felt. Let's go for a ride!

PART ONE

GUIDING FORCES

1 - THE EXPLOSION

I came on the scene in March of 1968. I was born in Rhode Island and still live here to this day. What I can share about the beginning of course is what was shared with me by my parents, aunts and uncles, and grandparents. I don't have the benefit of remembering anything before the age of five. I've been told that I was a peaceful baby. That all I did was eat and sleep and that I wasn't a bother to anyone, yet! A year and two days later my mother and father had my sister. She and I were very close growing up, not at all today.

From what I remember the four of us were a happy family. Mom, Dad, two children. A Saint Bernard named Whiskey. And a cat, Ramy. When you're young you have no choice but to be happy, you haven't been corrupted yet! Look about you. Observe the young ones, the children. Watch as they take in the splendor of the world through their eyes. Watch the innocence and the naivety that fuels their beings. It's just damn near perfection, as was my life.

I had the benefit of grandparents in my life. A maternal grandmother and grandfather, Nana and Papa. A fraternal grandmother, Moo. Yes, "Moo." I couldn't pronounce the Swedish word for grandmother and landed on "Moo." Being the eldest of her grandchildren I had the honor of giving her this name with my limited vocabulary.

The closest of my aunts and uncles were my father's siblings. His younger sister and younger brother, both of whom would take their turns as "parents" to and for me through life's consequences. More so my uncle. but my aunt later on in life when I would divorce my first wife. Yeah, what good story wouldn't have a good divorce or two mixed in?

We lived in a small home in a great neighborhood. A neighborhood with many families and many children. Though it was the smallest house on the street and we didn't own it, it was great. Until the shit hit the fan.

I was brought up from day one with the *idea* of God being instilled in me. I was told there was a God. That He was real, even though I couldn't *see* Him. That He did amazing things. Papa would refer to Him as the Grand Architect in later years when we said grace before a holiday dinner. We were a mixed bag of religions yet we all believed in God. I was brought up in the Catholic faith. As was my mother and her mother. Papa was a protestant. Nana the Irish catholic and Papa the English protestant. They married these two backgrounds when it was unheard of. Amazing how love will conquer all divisions, eh? Moo was a Lutheran and we all went to different churches. I guess somehow the argument was won that my sister and I would be brought up with the Catholic faith.

It fell on Nana to *follow through* with the Catholic teachings and to make sure we were brought to "God's house." I actually enjoyed it, I loved it. It was a reprieve from life for a bit and it always felt somewhat mystical when I was in the church. All that pomp and circumstance with the rituals and the smell of frankincense. Even to this day I'm taken by it to some degree when I'm in the midst of my work with clients and the beginning of their lives together at the altar through marriage.

So in the midst of being a child and going to elementary school and learning how to be a human in society with the other neighborhood children I had a mass to look forward to each week with Nana. She called me "pet" and I loved spending time with her.

Maybe it's clear to see how a young boy who is worshipped by a grandmother can turn that same grandmother into his own God. That is what she became and was, to and for me. She was larger than life in so many ways. I started drinking just before she died.

Long before this would happen a fuse was set in the family and I didn't even know that it was there. When you're a young child you don't see them. You observe innocence through a heart-shaped lens that is crystal clear. The fuse was between my parents. And when it was lit and the dynamite finally blew it sent shockwaves throughout the entire family. Sides were taken and lines were drawn. And in the midst of it all, my sister and I could only (fill in your own blank).

Before this there were arguments, easily ignored by me and my own childish agenda of what color to use next in that crayon box, my own need to figure out how to torch an ant with a magnifying glass and other things that interest a young boy. I was under the spell of that bliss that comes with being young, before outside forces have their chance to start the bastardation of the soul and mind. What I didn't see coming with the refusal to acknowledge these arguments was the devastating affect this would have on me. More to the point, how this explosion would set in motion the forming of *ideas, emotions, and attitudes* that would shape the *guiding forces* in my life. I was ill-prepared and what little understanding of God I had just wasn't enough to sustain me or fight them off. My trust and reliance on God as the Ultimate Source and Architect of all had yet to fully form. My understanding now is that all things, perceived good or bad, are put to great use by Him but it just wasn't there yet. Sadly it would be nearly forty-four years before I would reach this understanding. The day the split happened between my mother and father became the catalyst propelling me away from God for a number of years.

I recall it like this. I remember being in my bedroom. I think my sister was there, we shared a bedroom. My mother and father were at the other end of the house, only a short distance away. She in the kitchen and he in the living room. There was music on in the living room, an album playing on the turntable that was set upon the top of the big ass television. You know that 1970's tube set in a piece of cabinetry. The music was loud. And my mother asked my father to turn it down. That's the recollection of what the argument was about. Years later I would find out what it was really about. Isn't it always "the straw that breaks the camel's back?" It was the same way when I would split from my first wife later on in life.

As the argument continued I felt this strange thing happen within me. Something I never experienced before this time in my short life. I think I was six years old when it happened. I started to feel *fear* for the first time. At first it was in the form of a thought: "I hope that argument doesn't come down the hall into my bedroom."

And then the explosion. My mother screamed "Get out!" Words she would say to me years later just before I would go to live with my father at fourteen years old.

What happened? My father left. It was that simple.

And then what happened? In my physical world I couldn't tell you.

What happened within? I stopped believing in God. His mercy. And His love.

I don't blame my parents for this. I don't hold Nana in contempt for not teaching me more about God before this happened so that I would be better prepared. Life doesn't work like that. Life gets messy! And mine was about to get really messy with the lines that were drawn.

I can't recall what time of the year it was, what the weather was like or what I ate for dinner that night or even if I ate dinner. It feels like a blackout of sorts. I still to this day can't recall. What I can tell you is that this initial separation from God was not just born out of that fear I experienced at that moment. I've come to know that it was actually a *resentment*. A resentment toward God. Funny how one can be resentful toward God and that misaligned anger can feel as real as burning your hand under hot water yet we as humans have difficulty and resistance when it comes to loving this same God. Man how that fucking humanness gets in the way.

Sadly, my sister and I would become a couple of ping pong balls between my parents for the next few years and a device of their own need to control or be controlled. I'm not throwing my parents under the bus here. They had and did what they had to do much like every other person has had to do what had to be done with all that they had to work with. Our failure(s) as humans, imperfect and fallible forms of life, will dictate this as being so.

2 - INTERMEZZO NUMBER ONE

This brings me to that great resentment that served as my separation from God.

As I've shared, I believed in God. I have always believed in Something bigger than all of us. I was taught to believe in Him. And most likely from day one. From what I've gathered in an understanding of what happened, what separated me from Him, was learned through the process of recovery from alcohol and drugs, chiefly. There have been many other things that have lent their own depth to the understanding but it was through the twelve steps of Alcoholics Anonymous that it was brought to life for me and ultimately returned me to Him.

The principles that many try to understand and adapt to their lives within the halls of those church basement meetings are pretty powerful, they were for me. I'm not going to get all quotey with you. I will however try to impart what I came upon by referencing some of what these pioneers came upon as they too recovered from what those who have recovered since know as a full recovery of body and mind. (Yes, full recovery is possible.)

The greatest part of the process of recovery and becoming recover*ed* is that the directions are the same for all yet our experience and interpretation of that experience does vary. The journey is different for everyone yet the information uncovered about the mind and body of not only alcoholics, but humans who are not alcoholic, can be the same. As is the actual *result*. The re-connection to God and a new awareness, a God-consciousness.

The original piece of literature offered by the men and women who came about a way to recover from that often misunderstood sickness alcoholism, what is essentially a spiritual malady, speaks to resentment being an offender. They speak to it as being the beginning of spiritual disease. The actual drink, or drug, or whatever other vice comes into play whether it be gambling, sex, food, or fill in the blank is but a symptom of something deeper. A result of a cause. It's really not the problem. It is the result of the initial problem. It starts as a solution and becomes a detriment to the sufferer and all those around them. It was so with me.

The irony is that even once I was separated from the alcoholic and drugs, the symptom, I was still riddled with the cause. The spiritual sickness. The founders of this process knew and wrote to the fact that even when the symptom, the alcohol and drugs in my case, are removed, there is much more there in the way of sickness. They wrote that the removal of these substances is not enough and that it would only be addressing the surface of the problem, and hardly that.

So how did this resentment become that "number one offender" in my life?

I believe I was six years old when my mother screamed "Get out" to my father. And in that single moment came fear. Followed by my number one resentment. It wasn't against my mother for screaming at my father. It wasn't at my father for following her direction and leaving the house. It wasn't at the house. It wasn't at my sister, the sun, the moon or the stars. It was a resentment that I immediately copped toward God. And it happened in a split second.

One moment I was an innocent child, doing child things, dreaming child dreams, making child plans, looking forward to child things and enjoying a child's life. And in a split second I held God in contempt. As my life began to take a new direction at the mercy of those around me, a direction laced with fear and uncertainty, the sun grew dim, the moon grew colder, and the stars began to fall from heaven. Boom. Just like that!

This effect is not limited to alcoholics, drug addicts, sex addicts, food addicts, smokers, or coffee drinkers. It happens with nearly all of us. I'm not trying to speak for you personally as I believe we each have our own experience(s). Yet I say this as I have come to share this not only with those who hang out in church basements but those who are upstairs too. Humans are fallible, we are all susceptible to this separation. Look around you. Look at your own experience.

So what was the result of this separation? Well we will get into all of that as we continue to turn pages but the immediate affect was one of loss and one of gain. Whatever belief I had up until this point, nurtured by Nana, was tossed aside and a willful decision to hold God in contempt was made. Yes at six years old. And I didn't even know it. And then a further decision brought me to a place of living without God. More pointedly, a decision to stop seeking Him whether through teachings in the church or readings, prayer or meditation. I washed my hands of Him. The paradox here is that at some levels I *still* believed in Him yet wanted nothing to do with Him.

My attitude toward God was "You did this to me!" "You split my family up." "You shattered my childhood." Yet I didn't even know this happened when it happened. That was the first result of my decision born out of the resentment. An absolute bewilderment, a "not knowing" that would propel me into a life lived on a self-willed course. I would be a godless creature knowing there was a God while doing ungodly things with an attitude centered on only one thing. Me.

How did that resentment become my own number one offender? What I've come to know is that *I* was the offender. I offended God by turning *my back* on Him. By not trusting in Him and His own plan and use for everything. And that was one of the most bitter pills I ever swallowed when I uncovered this truth about myself years later. A taste that can still be experienced with even the shortest of trips down memory lane. I believe those bitter pills are a sort of discipline from God today and I'll touch on this later in the journey.

The brilliance of what the pioneers of that first twelve step program came upon is revealed right after they speak to this whole number one offender thing. They speak to the fact that if I can address this underlying malady, the spiritual sickness, I will then straighten out physically and mentally. And further that the *madness* of resentments can be *mastered.* Ultimately I would come to know that a resentment is simply my wish to be in total control no matter what the cost may be. And I became willing to pay that price, to the point of near ruin.

I could write chapters about my history in Alcoholics Anonymous but that is for another day yet there will be points I'll reference here. When I got sober through a treatment facility and was exposed to the fellows in those church basements I was exposed to a great many things that served as revelations to me. One of which was what they told many of us back in the 1980's. They spoke about how this illness, alcoholism, takes hold. They said the "order" in which one gets sick is spiritual, mental and then physical. They then shared that the exact reversal in order was true when we recover. They were somewhat right yet misguided in their approach. I waited year after year to get better in the reverse order. And to no avail. Sure, at first I felt great physically and then my mind did begin to clear, a bit. And then I waited for the spiritual part to get better. The wait nearly killed me, and those about me.

It wasn't until I was twenty-six years sober attending meeting after meeting after meeting doing what I was told to do before I landed at a decision to take my own life, going so far as dry firing a pistol in my mouth to practice. All the while waiting for that miracle. It was bullshit.

The pioneers knew what they spoke to in their first book. That if the spiritual malady is overcome, my physical life, not just my body but the physical aspects of my life would right themselves on their own. That if the spiritual malady is overcome my mind will repair itself; a restoration of sanity. Sound reasoning would prevail in my life instead of the twisted and perverse mental streak I endured for years. My mind would look upon all things, most especially God, with a different eye. And this became my exact experience.

Do you hold God in contempt?

After a great many years of doing so myself I was able to gain a reconnection to God. Yes, the process hurt and required a concentrated effort but it beat the alternative, blowing my head off and leaving my family behind in their own twisted bewilderment.

I love this little bit that I heard once. But before I share it with you let me tell you how I understand this relationship with God in its simplest form. I look upon him as my Parent and I'm simply His child. There is so much more and I'll get into that as we travel on but for now let's leave it there. Simple.

So He's the parent and I'm the kid. And like most kids I've done things that are colorful and distasteful. Who hasn't? Now I have my own children and I'm a parent too so I get what it's like to be a parent. You're a parent too? Not always easy is it, being a parent? But no matter what your own children do it never ceases to amaze how the love for your children is felt. It's deep! And they give us trouble as many of you have given your parents trouble, as I have given my parents trouble. This brings us to two points.

One. Parents and children love one another. It is innate, unavoidable. And children give their parents trouble, heartache, and headaches.

And Two. You think you're having a problem

with God? Maybe as a parent He's having a problem with you. I imagine He had His hands quite full with me. Actually, today I know He did.

3 - DEBRIS

As I made my way into a new space of trying to figure out what the hell happened there was much confusion and many questions. One day I'm eating donuts on a Sunday morning from Mister Donut with my father and sister and the next thing I know I'm only allowed to see him on Wednesday nights and for a few hours on a Sunday.

And then of course there's that entire thinking that accompanies most children at a young age when their parents get divorced. Thoughts along the line of "This is my fault." "I did something wrong." And then the granddaddy of them all, "I'm defective and unlovable." Basically I took on the responsibility for their divorce. I think it's almost natural and it becomes part of our constitution.

My father quickly remarried and my mother fell to pieces. My father's new marriage came with a set of her own children from her divorce. This compounded that "I'm defective" line of thought and I truly believed I was tossed aside and traded in for a newer model.

Had it not been for my mother's parents, Nana and Papa, I believe my sister and I would have been totally fucked. My mother tried as hard as she could to keep it together. She worked and put on the usual routine within our home as best she could. She just didn't have the Power to keep trudging without a fall.

I remember the first Christmas without my father. The tree went up, was decorated and some gifts even appeared below it. But it didn't feel like Christmas to me. I recall walking about the house with the hope that my father would walk through the door any moment and compliment the tree. We would all be reunited by Santa's grace. It never happened. You guessed it. "Fuck you Santa!"

That's the funny thing about that number one resentment. It likes a snowball that is rolled to create a snowman's head. It gets bigger on its own and builds as it rolls forward. This was my experience with the number one resentment against God. It became a compounded mess of more and more resentments. And the fact that these would begin to occupy my mind and heart at a deeper level had a detrimental effect.

These effects served only to block me further from God. They began to cause delusions. I began to start imagining things. Not voices in my mind, well maybe a touch. Delusions, false opinions, false beliefs. My mind took a turn for the worse and neither I, nor anyone in the family, noticed it.

Mix with this the need to be a part of, to be recognized and seen, mostly by my parents, all sorts of other defects of character began to take shape. They are born like we are and grow much like we do.

At six years old I became a liar. Fueled by delusion and imagination, this ability to lie extended to nearly every word I managed to get out. I began to believe these lies, my own lies, and thought others did as well. My teachers, my friends, and their parents, my parents and my grandparents. I became a storyteller and as I believed my own "stories" the delusion grew deeper.

All of this formed a foundation for a life of behaviors that would inspire a "look at me" or "look what I did" position. I wanted and needed to be the center of attention. I wanted and needed to be the best at everything I did. The latter is not always a bad thing yet when born out of this delusional way of thinking it had no chance of ending well.

As much as my parents enjoyed their own game of control or be controlled I had my part and grew very skilled at the play of this game. My mother once called me a "self-centered manipulative bastard." Ouch! And that was the role I gladly accepted with ignorance.

By the time I was in second grade, seven years old, I quickly learned how to manipulate those about me with laughter or a few tears. I recall my second grade teacher, Miss DeMizio, catching me change a name on another classmate's handwriting assignment. That's how delusional I became in just one year. I actually thought my script matched his. Mine was a complete mess compared to his near-perfection. When I was cornered, caught, I quickly reverted to tears with a sob story about how my mother and father had split and I was out late with my father the night before. The result? I got away with it. Naturally. The lesson learned? When cheating, balance the weight of consequences with a plan to avert them.

Now you might think I'd learn a lesson and walk away from a life of deceit. Negative. The experience only seemed to bolster that triumphant feeling of "See what I did."

The thing is this. I lost that authentic self that was seeking God and chose to embrace that other self, the ego.

What a trip to be able to have that conversation with my second grade teacher years later and to come clean about it. I think it took me by surprise more so than her as my recollection and amend for what I did verbally left me before I even knew what was happening. It was met with compassion and laughter.

4 - INTERMEZZO NUMBER TWO

The often looked over, skimped upon, and dismissed principle in the twelve steps is that of the amends process. The principle of going out to those you have hurt trying to set things straight. It's not easy and can be wrapped up in fear but as one who has walked into the most brutal of them I can testify that the worth in this part of the process described with words here will fall far short. (I've witnessed countless people fail to follow through in this area and ultimately land back on the drink, or worse, become a messier shipwreck.)

Now why would I want to bring this up in this part of the writing and what does this have to do with where we are in the story at this point? It was an experience with one of the most difficult amends I had to make that fits here and speaks directly to what another has observed in me my entire life, even if only from afar.

I mentioned that my father quickly remarried and that this marriage came with a set of children that were introduced to me as my "step sisters." From the very start I tried to curry favor with my new step mother. It never worked. I knew it and she knew it.

Words did not have to be spoken between us to express this, it just wasn't there between us. Have you ever had a relationship where no words had to be spoken, where the lack of words clearly defined the roles and depth, or lack of depth, in the relationship? It was like that between her and I.

As much as neither one of us cared for each other there were times in my life where I hurt this women. Sometimes it was not intentional and at others it indeed was. As ironic as it is that she would be the one amends that I would learn the most from she would also be the one "parent" that I would learn the most from. Talk about a paradox.

Step nine calls for the direct amends to those we have harmed and this must be done without harming others in the process. This can be a slippery proposition and a bit of wiggle room is there to hedge if you ask me, yet this feature is clearly important.

When I came out of the process of these steps, the heavy lifting part, the self-examination and sharing of what was found, I set out to tackle that long list of people that needed to be approached. Naturally my parents were on the top of the list. I called my father to arrange a time for us to meet. There was going to be a 50/50 shot on whether he would agree to meet. I placed the call and he said he would think about it and call me back. Who could blame him? I'd been ambushing the poor bastard my entire life with blame and contempt. He probably felt an immediate need to protect himself.

The call came a day or so later and he agreed to meet with me. Being fresh out of the process with an experience I never had before, an immediate reconnection to God and a pretty explosive spiritual upheaval, and being a novice at this amends process with that underlying God-consciousness I never thought to ask, include, or invite his wife into the meeting. I didn't realize this until I walked into the front door of their home.

I was full of fear as I drove the hour and a half there. I listened to soothing music to try and calm my spirit. I was going to come clean for nearly a lifetime of *wrongs* and what amounted to a mountain of bullshit I put him through. It might even cost me money, and of course I still carried the fear of rejection and the idea that what others thought of me was significant.

As I pulled into their driveway everything in me, the old me that was quickly being tossed aside, screamed "What are you fucking crazy going in there? Run. Turn around. Go home to your wife and children." The death of the ego is downright nasty; it's like an exorcism. But there was Something Else there I couldn't see or touch, but I definitely felt It. And a peace came over me as I opened the door of my truck to go in.

As I walked to the door and went in I was filled with panic. I never thought to include my step mother and felt as though I already failed.

Once we parted ways with talk about the drive up and the weather she began to dismiss herself and made ready to leave. Something inside, a voice, an intuitive part that speaks to us at times very clearly and even loudly, pleaded with me to invite her into the conversation. She agreed to stay. I'll never know why she did. Maybe it was simply curiosity.

As I began to lay out why I was there and the purpose of my visit it became easier to come clean for those many times I fell short in being a decent son and step son. A decent human being.

The many times I stole their pot. The gold chain I stole. The many times I lied to them. The many times I treated them with no respect. And on and on it went.

Now here's the thing about living a life of spiritual sickness disconnected from God and trying to manage life, your thoughts and actions, on your own. Those delusions and lies we tell ourselves and the guilt, shame, and remorse that builds like that snowball grows to an insurmountable mountain of rubble. The damage left in my wake was pretty drastic. I'll be paying for it one way or another for the rest of my life. It is a small price to pay as you will see.

As I finished the door was opened for them to hold my feet to the fire. This is where the amends became uncomfortable but lent so much useful information to my transformation. My father went first and told a story about when he was twelve years old and a situation between he and his own father. It was a parable of sorts. I can't remember the meat of it but can recall the effect. My impression was that he passed forgiveness to me.

Way back at the beginning of this journey I spoke to guiding forces being set by what is handed to us and what is formed by us in the way of those ideas, emotions, and attitudes. It was during the next part as my feet were held to the fire by my step mother that I clearly had this concept defined for me.

I mentioned that gold chain. I remember I stole this from the two of them when I was a teenager. I didn't even know why at the time. Spite? Yeah, that might be it. I took it, that's what I did. We will revisit this item later on in the story.

I was always accused of taking the chain, rightly so, but my position was that of denial and I came to believe that I didn't do it. When I came clean for this with the two of them and offered to make financial reparation for it the delusion I had been living with including the attendant shame and remorse was shattered. I was always told that the chain was a gift from my step mother's ex-husband and had sentimental value. On this particular day as I came clean and was being cleansed the truth was that my father and step mother bought the chain hot from another person. It had no sentimental value and through their own grace they would not accept payment for it.

I can put off the next part of what took place but this is why I brought you to this Intermezzo. The greatest takeaway of what I experienced as a young child was that I thought I was defective. And what do most of us do with something that is irregular or defective? We cover it up. We put a mask on it in an attempt to change its front. It's look. This is what I began doing at a young age. I put a mask on and the effort after that was to keep the mask in place.

Now my father shared a simple story and all was cleared between us, for a time. Now it was my step mother's turn to hold my feet to the fire. This was an hour long session of many statements on her part. Accusations some dead on and of which I took full responsibility for. Some were far off the mark and there was a sense of celebration within when I could rightly deny those. And then there were numerous questions. All of this took place in three 20 minute sessions with her taking a cigarette break in between.

After the first twenty minutes of being hammered something amazing happened. I felt the Grace of God. I know this because I did not want to harm her, not even with a slap. The second twenty minutes saw more statements and a comment to the effect that she had been waiting for my "mask to fall off" for years. There it was!

Now after about forty minutes or so of this conversation I became more and more at peace. My father on the other hand did not. He was becoming visibly uncomfortable. As his wife went outside to smoke he asked me if I still smoked. I said I did and he looked at me with a look that pleaded "Don't you want to have a cigarette at this point?" I declined and said I was good. If you're a smoker you know that this is probably the most opportune time to do so. I felt good and besides she was telling me something of myself that I clearly needed to hear. And needed to understand about spiritual sickness at a deeper level.

Her third time at the table brought about some declarative statements that landed in this realm.

"I never wanted you as a son and never will."

"I never liked you and never wanted to like you."

"I never loved you and never wanted to love you."

Now I know I may still have been under the spell of some delusional thinking but I'm confident that this is what I heard. The wording may not be exact but it is most definitely what I inferred. This came out in the last twenty minutes of our meeting and as she made her way outside to smoke another cigarette, and a possible reload, I felt a kick within that told me "It's time to leave this place, you have done your part." Besides it was becoming a bashing session at this point, something I no longer accept.

I told my father I had to go and started to put my coat on. By the time my step mother returned my hat and gloves were on. I was able to thank them for their time. And before I left that intuitive kick propelled me to ask if I could call on them in the future. The reply was yes. And then out of nowhere I asked my step mother if I could give her a hug. Now that's not a normal reaction to what just took place. It's signs like this that tell me there is a God and if He is sought remarkable things will happen, *if* I can match His favor with effort. This has been my experience as you will see.

ROBERT ERNEST BACH

5 - THE BURGER KING

Here's one to chew on for a moment. "What is normal for the spider is absolute chaos for the fly." I don't know who said it but isn't it true?

Before the dynamite blew my family apart I lived the life of a spider in a tight web, comfortable and secure in the fact that all was well and I was safe. And then all of a sudden I was the fly. It was not a slow and easy switch in perception. It was sudden, and violent.

My grandmother, Nana, was my rock, my own personal higher power. One in whom I could place absolute trust and reliance. She defended me. She went to the wrestling mat for me on more than one occasion. She spoiled me rotten and tried everything in her own power to make my life easier. She gave me everything she had in her and when she died a galaxy-sized piece of me went with her. I was 12 years old.

As I tried to navigate these sudden changes in my life, and my thinking, she stepped up and stepped in as my mother in many respects. As my mother tried in all earnest to keep going, before finally tossing in her own towel, I spent every weekend with Nana.

My sister and I were brought to Nana and Papa's home, or they came and picked us up. The weekend became the focal point for me throughout the week. When I was troubled with fits of rage and anger I learned to suppress, more on that one later, the thought of going there on the weekend would keep me going. The same when sadness and indecision came about. Nana. Focal point. Everything will be okay. The weekend is coming.

We would arrive on a Friday night, my mother was waiting tables and worked on Friday and Saturday nights, and we would stay through the weekend. A mass at church was nearly mandatory on the Saturday afternoon or the Sunday morning depending on her preference I suppose. Papa never came with us. Funny how the "guys" got away with skipping this part of life. Most times we would attend a Sunday morning mass before returning for a large home-cooked breakfast at the kitchen table, always with lots of bacon and warm Italian bread. And tea. With lots of sugar. And milk.

When we left their house later in the morning we went one of two places depending on the whims of my mother and father. You never knew which way the wind was going to blow until Sunday morning. We would either head back home to the other side of the city. Back to reality. Or we would be retrieved at their house by my father for his Sunday visitation. Noon until 5pm. On one rare occasion we were allowed to sleep at his place. On that occasion I felt free. As free as he must have felt after the divorce. It was new and like anything new there is always a degree of excitement. Colors are more vivid and sharper and smells seem more fragrant.

It may seem as though I'm getting away from the topic but before I go back let's travel deeper into the scene that took place in the apartment that served as another attitude that set up my guiding forces. As I learned to navigate these new waters and territories I still had the ability to ask hard questions. You know, the way children "say the darnedest things." And ask the "darnedest questions."

I can recall spending the night at my father's apartment. A two bedroom place in a building loaded with other tenants, and smells. We woke to bowls of Fruit Loops and The Beatles on the turntable. The album about the walrus. As we got ready for the day and enjoyed that feeling of "being together" my sister was in the bathroom brushing her teeth. She had this cool way of smiling that always made me smile. The air at Dad's place felt light. It felt alive! I believe the word I'm looking for is hopeful. Yeah, it was like a hot air balloon filled with hope and I recall that the sun was shining.

Now I've covered two of the attributes I picked up immediately upon my parent's separation. The part of that mask I'll label the "liar." And then of course there was the "cheat." We brushed against the "thief" and we will circle back there shortly but before we do there is that one underlying element that would prevent me from seeking answers in my life for a great many years and on the other side of that coin came the need to just do it my way without seeking advice or counsel. An explosive and necessary additive to anyone who lives a life propelled by self-will.

Burger King. Now let me say this, I agreed that broiling beat frying when it came to burgers and it helped that you could see them make their way over the flames by way of a metal conveyer belt. This was when their fries were pretty good too. Too much opinion there, my apologies.

The point here is that this was a different time when fast food wasn't so fast and eating with some kind of decorum was still en vogue. Well, as much as it could be in a burger joint. They allowed you to use real silverware. There were glass salt and pepper shakers on the tables along with that glass cube of different sweeteners. Now if the four of us sat down together there were four sets of silverware that we ate with. The restaurant never saw this silverware again. It was quickly shoved into Nana's pocketbook. And for good measure she would help herself to the sugars and salt and pepper shakers. Needless to say but when you opened the drawer that held the flatware at Nana and Papa's home none of it matched. It came from all different restaurants that were visited. Maybe this was just the way it was back in the 1970's but years later I would be working an event and an installation at a hotel or country club. After my client would carefully put together a "headache basket" for the benefit of the female guests and place it in the ladie's restroom, I would witness what I came to call the "slow-moving blue cloud," those elderly ladies who always seemed to have a blue tint to their freshly made hair styles, their own personal armor, enter these areas and fill their bags as if toothpaste and hand cream were never going to be produced again.

The ideas and concepts we adapt at a young age that are sometimes skillfully, most times unknowingly, dictated to us, first by our immediate family, rippled inward toward us from our friends, teachers and administrators and whoever else we are exposed to is never-ending. It's a constant barrage against our conscience.

From the most powerful person in my life I learned that it was okay to take what you wanted whether you needed it or not. Regretfully my life and that mask would include this fierce element.

As my sister and I learned to maneuver through these changes the greatest fear was that of *doing without*. And one of mine was putting myself in a place of someone in the family taking their love away. I had already learned that it can be turned off and even I have been guilty of doing the same in my life.

Mom tried to the best of her ability to maintain some sense of normalcy in her own way and at times this became creative. Each year we would get the Christmas tree although it was never the same for me until later on in life when I had my own children. Even then I would put it up and decorate it waiting for the miracle of love, stability, and normalcy to return to my mind.

My mother had this wreath. It was a variety that was made out of pine cones only, no greens. Very plain yet full. She would hang this on the front door every year and I suppose that one year it needed a new bow. Maybe the one that was on it was weak and tired looking. Or maybe it was the lure of another one down the street. Imagine being a child and being driven down the street to steal a bow off of a memorial stone in your neighborhood. Now imagine doing it in broad daylight. Now imagine you are the parent and you drive your children down the street to steal this bow for you. This is what my mother insisted we do and heaven forbid I don't follow her direction. She might turn off that "I love you" switch.

This became normal for me. The taking of what I wanted. When I wanted it.

And this was not limited to physical items. Stealing your feelings and heart became child's play for me. I told you my mother called me a "self-centered manipulative bastard" when I was growing up. She was not off the mark there. It is one of the defining characteristics of alcoholics. The irony is that it became my character long before I picked up a drink.

A short time later I was pinched stealing candy from the local 7-Eleven. They had this entire aisle of nothing but candy. No coincidence that heaven rhymes with their name. The bottom shelf of this glorious gateway to sugar was what we called "penny candy." And there were so many varieties. Stealing money from my mother's bag became natural and I loved to fill a bag with this penny candy. I remember walking into the store and filling the counter with candy and handing the cashier money. And then with zero thought I turned back to the candy aisle and added more candy to my bag while the cashier watched me! She stopped me as I made to leave the store and called me on it.

I wanted to explain to her that it was perfectly fine for me to do this. I was shown, basically already taught, that it was okay to do this. Yet something in her expression created a resistance within, something like "It's not going to work." There weren't consequences for my actions. Just that big person telling a small person not to do it again. In my mind the lesson became "I would have to be more careful the next time I stole something."

ROBERT ERNEST BACH

6 - YES SIR!

The upside of losing the ability to ask questions is that you learn to figure things out on your own. This does have some advantages. Years ago I read that whimsical yet tight book titled "Who Moved My Cheese?" I've since shared this title with many other men that I have worked with. I even handed it to my children as they were growing up.

The gist of the story is that we have a choice in our approach to everything. As explained in the book we can either "hem" or "haw" and find a reason not to do something. Or we can "scratch" or "sniff" our way to a viable solution or ending.

Papa was a World War II veteran and proud of his service to our country. That service to his fellows didn't end when he was discharged. He believed in helping the weak, empowering them by showing them how to do whatever it was that needed to be done. And mostly by his own example or a demonstration of how to do it.

This is what it was like for me growing up with

shown at a young age what the damages of drinking to excess or alcoholically can do. Yet I was intrigued by it. The drinking. There was a fascination that would grow in me.

My father could turn a 16 ounce Ballantine Ale can into a planter by shredding the can and curling the cut aluminum. We had one hanging in the kitchen window in our home. Alcohol was always a big part of any family gathering. Some in the family could handle it squarely but some not so much. This I can see with the benefit of hindsight where vision is nearly always 20/20.

During the summer my sister and I would travel to Papa's sister and husband's house out in Chepachet on the pond. We would play all day in the water, in the sand, and on the dock. The adults would sit around and drink hi-balls all day. Clearly they got happier and happier as the day went on but some would not be as happy by the end of the day. It's not my position to say who might have had a problem with alcohol. I know I had a problem. And I place no store in the thinking that alcoholism is genetic. My experience in recovery has taught me differently. It is not a genetic thing.

Papa was forever the Master Sergeant. You didn't screw with him, at all. Unless of course you had Nana on your side to protect you. Papa was a generous man. Generous in praise and instruction. Generous in support, in life and financially. And he always encouraged me to do and be the absolute best that I could be in whatever I chose to do. Always with the directive "If you're not going to give it your best and do it right don't waste another's time." And you thought all that I was going to share with you was going to be the underbelly, the side many don't want to look at?

Not so. As I have said I need to lay out before you all of the different ideas, the different emotions and the different attitudes that were freely handed to me, mostly in an absent-minded fashion by others, that would *set up* those guiding forces. The *guiding forces* that would determine the course in my own life. Please remember I made that choice to bring about all that would take place in my life. I was, and am, the only one responsible for it. I always had the choice based on my level of consciousness to change my direction. At least until I started drinking and doing drugs. I could have returned to God anytime I wanted to. And on some levels and in some perverse way deep down inside I *knew* that I should do just that. I just didn't know how. It was like I had rowed out into the middle of that pond in a canoe and I was at the mercy of a strong headwind that kept turning my canoe in the opposite direction as I sat in the rear seat. The needed power was not there to affect a change. And wouldn't be for three decades.

I have to share this last part with you before we turn another page in my story.

Papa made a deal with my sister and I as we entered elementary school. For each "A" that was earned in school we received a dollar. We got 50 cents for a "B." And this would happen for each quarter throughout the school year. He instilled what it meant in the way of value and how to work for something. My perverted and twisted thinking, already formed, was cunning.

My sister and I would fish off the end of the dock with poles and balled up bread. We fished for sunfish, the ones with the spot on the side of them. We earned money for each fish that we caught. If by chance we caught a pickerel or horned pout we earned more. Maybe you can guess my aim and goal here. Earn in the quickest and easiest manner. Not something that was handed to me in the form of an idea from anyone in the family. I was starting to form my own ideas based on my already peculiar train of thought. The problem was getting deeper now and I was still years away from drinking.

I quickly learned that if you spread the crumbs on the top of the water you attracted a plethora of sunfish almost immediately and with a net the earnings were quick. And with all of the activity of the sunfish, the horned pout, the real bread winner, was sure to arrive.

I made a lot of money fishing when I was a child of elementary school age.

I also knew when to do it. I mean I knew how many hi-balls in I'd have to wait before my move.

7 - INTERMEZZO NUMBER THREE

I started attending Alcoholics Anonymous meetings immediately upon entering a treatment facility at the age of eighteen. I was exposed to those twelve steps you may have heard about in the same manner, from the very start. In fact I was told I would go through those twelve steps or they, the fellows of the first group I joined, would "shoot my kneecaps off." Yeah, brutal. It was the 1980's and they didn't believe in the warm and fuzzy approach, at least in the area of the world I was in. I'll go back to the shooting of the kneecaps later on. And the idea of skydiving to find God.

The first step requires an admission of powerlessness over alcohol. That's the simplest form of the first part of that step. And the understanding and acceptance of that was equally as simple for me to understand. I was beaten into submission by alcohol, and drugs. I understood the powerlessness. The inability to choose whether or not to drink. The inability to stop drinking once I started. There will be more on this later on in the journey for us to contemplate.

The second part of that first step, its full implication, would be lost on me for years into recovery. It simply suggests that my life has become unmanageable. The surface implication of this *teaching* resonated with me. My life certainly did become unmanageable, downright messy, as a result of my drinking.

The effects of drinking permeated every fiber of my being and every fiber of those closest to me. At the age of eighteen my life was in shambles. I was forced to leave high school two weeks before I was due to graduate. I settled for a GED which I achieved when I left treatment. I was having difficulty with personal relationships, family, friends, teachers, employers and so on. Where alcohol once allowed me to control my emotional nature as though it was a medication, it now failed miserably. And speaking of misery it was all I felt within and all I could see, without. Those ugly trees. Depression, dark and ominous, sank nearly every one of my days. Making a living or earning money became impossible as I became that impossible employee. I felt like a useless piece of crap and thoughts of taking my own life became sort of a frequent reprieve from reality. I was not happy in the least. I couldn't help myself and was of no help to others though I always tried to emanate that spirit of being helpful that I watched Papa demonstrate.

I could easily relate to a life that had grown unmanageable and could see that all of it was the result of the alcohol. Pretty convenient when you can blame, hold accountable, someone or something for a boatload of *symptoms*. Now here's the part of this important first step I wouldn't come to understand for years the way I see it today.

Before I take this idea of unmanageability further please allow me to state that I do not represent any twelve step program. I do speak on theirs or anyone else's behalf. Or their interpretation of those steps or recovery. This entire body of my writing is laced with only my interpretation of these principles. Each travels their own path and comes to their own understanding. If this book helps you to understand something about you or your thinking, maybe even your drinking or whatever vice you might use as a form of escape from reality at a deeper level then so be it. If not, then so be it.

I actually do believe in those laws of attraction. I may not fully understand them yet can clearly see their power. I believe like attracts like and that water does seek its own level. My *life* is based on thought. My life is the direct result of a thought. Each one of my thoughts leads to a decision. And that decision will determine my course, my actions. Or even my inaction. I just made a cup of coffee while I stepped away from my laptop. As I sat here typing the previous paragraph I thought "I would like a cup of coffee." I made a decision to get up and make a cup of coffee. I then followed this with the action of getting up to make a cup of coffee. My immediate "life" became what I thought of. I'm now enjoying a cup of coffee while I share with you.

My understanding of an unmanageable life today is that it's not the outside, the tangible aspects of my life, that were unmanageable but my thoughts. It was not the unmanageability in my life caused by alcohol only. The resultant unmanageability caused by my abuse of alcohol was real yet it all came down to a corruption that began to take place at an age that I've been describing to you in the previous chapters. My life, my surroundings and my reactions to them all began with one thought. That I could be my own life manager. Well I don't know about you or your life, your thoughts, or your situation, past or present, but I failed at the thinking game. And failed miserably.

And I came to an understanding that as long as my thoughts are corrupt my outside life and its appearance, my reactions to you and circumstances, and overall approach to life will be an extension of this. Corrupted and uncomfortable. Unmanageable.

And the more corrupt and unmanageable my thoughts the more harm I do to myself, my family and you. Even though I was sober as you will come to find out.

I have nothing but praise for that initial piece of literature the founders of Alcoholics Anonymous published in 1939. How could I not when my own experience decades after its publication came to match theirs identically just by following the directions contained within?

I share my "story" with many others who have had this near identical experience and we each explore its fruits with one another on a regular basis. As well as our experiences and interpretations of this literature as it pertains to both our individual and collective journeys. There are many schools of thought when it comes to trying to decipher what was written decades ago and these schools have different grades. Some in the recovery community may not like that last statement. Maybe they are not in the same place in their understanding as I, as many others are, though we all share the same roof.

For instance, there is a bit that speaks to the way one's life, thoughts, will become if they can endure the heavy lifting *required* to have their sound reasoning restored. Their sanity. These are fondly called by many the "promises." For years, even I referred to them as promises. I've come to know that these "promises" are actually the new set of conditions I will experience in my life.

Some of us who have recovered our sanity, recovered from that condition of hopelessness as it pertains to the body and mind, and more to the point have recovered a God-consciousness we lost through one simple decision long before we turned to the drink, and have had that subsequent further deepening of a relationship with God, refer to these promises as *predictions*. They are but only a partial result of the *necessary* work for any real alcoholic who is willing to take concentrated *action* to recover. If none of this makes any sense to you, that's perfectly fine. Perhaps the next part will and may give you a clearer understanding of why I'm even writing and cataloging all of this telling look at my own life and experience, my spiritual experience that would transform my life and even those close to me.

One of these predictions is that we come to know that our own experience in life, not just recovery, can and will benefit others. And ironically the farther down my fall the more benefit my own experience can be. For you. For me. And for God.

Which brings me to my next point before we make a return to those three magical ingredients, ideas, emotions, and attitudes, that set up all of the guiding forces in my life as we look at one other relationship in my life before I move forward to further recklessness.

Before I go any deeper here please allow me the latitude to declare that I am not a doctor. I am not a therapist with models to work from. I'm just your average drunk who got sober and has experience working with others for years now and have become fully acquainted with the insidiousness of this illness, this spiritual sickness. A familiarity with my own and with many other's.

The real alcoholic is defined by two key components. The first component is rather simple. It's the concept of the *body allergy*. Something happens in the alcoholic once alcohol *in any form* is introduced into the body, the blood stream. To this day science does not know why once alcohol is introduced to the physical body it sets off a craving in some people. It is something that cannot be explained. It is called the phenomenon of craving.

It is far more palatable to accept the man, woman or child who suffers from a peanut allergy. And their adverse physical reaction is nearly identical, its immediate. The readiness to assist this person is easily forthcoming. It is the same concept with the alcoholic yet the alcoholic's actions or inactions seem to always bring fierce misunderstanding and even resentment. It's difficult to understand this sickness unless one has it. (This is why one alcoholic can help another when no one can. This is just a quick synopsis here, I'll expand on this in later chapters.)

The second component is the one that seems to baffle not only the alcoholic but all those around the sufferer. It's the *mind* of the alcoholic and many chapters can be written on this yet to get to the broader point judiciously I'll keep this part simple as well. The mind of the alcoholic is screwed up. It's like a mental illness. Sound reasoning has been displaced by a peculiar way of thought. The foremost in the mind being "This time I'll control it." or "It won't hurt me this time." Even though the last time a drink was had there was nothing but damage and suffering all about. The alcoholic can't recall that before the choice is made to have a drink. The alcoholic mind is foggy.

It doesn't have to be a broken shoe lace or a stubbed toe. It doesn't have to require a cause for celebration. It doesn't have to be a sunny day. Or a rainy day. A bad day or a great day. Once the idea is there to take a drink, all bets are off. They are off and running. And as I said, once alcohol hits that bloodstream and that phenomenon kicks in there is no stopping. This is what it was like for me when I drank. The only way I could stop was by either passing out or running out of it. But like most severe alcoholics I always had a backup plan and always had a stash in case I did run out. Alcoholics are a resourceful bunch. I was.

When I got sober the idea that I would need to find some kind of Power greater than myself was not an easy pill to swallow. It was bitter. Yet I was desperate. And hopeless. So much so that I'd try anything at all to get and stay sober. And muster up the value for a set of kneecaps and a willingness to try something different than what I was doing.

For me the idea of finding this Power was easily digestible when it came to my alcohol problem. It was even easy to ask for help and assistance from this Power as long as it was limited to my problem(s) with alcohol. The difficulty I had was in letting go of all of those old ideas, emotions, and attitudes which in turn made it nearly impossible to break free from those guiding forces. For the longest time I believed *I* could tackle these issues on my own. I was wrong. The needed power was not there.

The very simple idea set forth in the book *Alcoholics Anonymous* through the findings of those original pioneers of this recovery process is lost on many today in the halls of these meetings. (If you're in recovery I just stirred that "seething cauldron of debate.") I can testify to this as this was my experience as well. This explosive piece of literature was never shared with me through the ignorance of others. It wasn't their fault, they were just passing on what was given to them.

This original piece of literature is affectionately called the "Big Book." No need to bore you with how it got that name. I was told that this Big Book had two purposes when I asked about it. One, if you can't sleep at night, read it, and it will put you to sleep. Two, if you can't get to a meeting in the course of a day read the stories in the back of the book, it would be like going to a meeting.

That very simple idea and finding that the pioneers came upon? That once a drinker has become a *real alcoholic* they have most likely placed themselves in a position of being "beyond human aid." The trick is for the alcoholic to find out if this is indeed so for themselves. I had to and it was true. Not one person can have this told to them. They, like I, need to discover the validity of this idea. The great part is that it is rather simple to do.

The extent to which I placed myself beyond human aid was not limited to my use or problem with alcohol. It extended to damn near every area of my life. As I grew older and maybe wiser and began to see the madness of my thoughts I set out to try and fix myself. I tried to adjust my thinking. I tried and tried and tried. And failed and failed and failed. There were many ways I tried to repair myself and most times I tried from the outside in. The fact of the matter is that it had to start from within. And it did. That combustion from within came shortly after my own practice of dry firing my pistol into my mouth. It came on the heels of a morning when I combat-rolled out of bed and begged God to "Please come get me. Please come take me home."

That petition was answered. Quickly. And not the way one would expect it to be.

I actually thought He would send a limousine to gather me up with a bouquet of flowers and a card message that read "You tried so hard. Okay, you can come home now."

It didn't happen that way.

I was twenty-six years sober when this happened.

I had to venture into that garden of good and evil.

I had to go through that "dark night of the soul" to gain freedom from the bondage of self and the ego.

ROBERT ERNEST BACH

8 - A BLACK DRESS

My basic constitution, my nature, formed at a young age, was to *not* ask questions. To not make waves. I had that fear that if I did I would be deemed unlovable and unworthy, that whatever capacity for love that my family had would be turned off. That's a legitimate fear considering the level of sensitivity I had and my reaction to that explosion from the dynamite.

It seems as though I have only been scratching the underbelly of my childhood, and so it has been. The underbelly was tempered by the topside at times. Creating a level of further confusion. I mentioned the effect Papa had on me with his work ethic and spirit of helpfulness and this has had a lasting effect on me up to this day.

"Moo" was another example of a strong female role model. The mother of my father she was one tough woman and she had her own battle scars from life. Who doesn't right? She didn't take any crap and said what was on her mind without reservation. This always caused arguments as it flowed in contradiction to that typical "don't talk, don't trust, don't cry" that many families have had passed onto them by previous generations. Crazy way of balancing out the two opposing forces.

This is where one of the strongest lines was drawn after the explosion. It was revealed many years later in my life as she and I enjoyed a renewed relationship based on a common situation between us. The drink.

In conversations during our daily visits we would explore our pasts, mutual and individual, looking for what could be gained by looking backwards. We would speak to the great memories we had at the beach eating hard-boiled eggs that were carefully wrapped in foil that she always brought to the shore in her cooler. The times she would pick me up at the ungodly hour of four in the morning to go deep-sea fishing. The time my fishing pole slid against the rail on the boat and wiped her eyeglasses off of her face and all we could do was watch them fall into the drink. (Her subsequent visit to get new glasses revealed a disorder in her eyes and it was a good thing this happened that day.) The time she promised to take my sister and I to the local feast near her apartment and the fact that she forgot this promise when my sister and I arrived at her place.

Nana and Papa attempted to drop us off at her apartment building and she didn't answer the buzzer when I rang. I saw that the sliding glass door was cracked open on her deck and knew I could climb up and get in. I think I was seven or eight years old and I remember the look in Papa's eyes as I monkeyed my way up. I let myself in and she was passed out in bed. I managed to wake her up and remind her of our plans and she responded by getting up and fulfilling the promise. All my life I just wanted relationships with my family members.

During one of our daily get-togethers, I was in my mid-twenties when these started, she revealed one of the granddaddy pieces of information that resolved so many unanswered questions that I had. I didn't ask the question that produced the answer, she offered, and I believe she was trying to set the record straight for herself.

The explosion between my parents produced so many changes and the one that had the greatest sting was about to be explained to me in a matter of fact way. She offered that after the divorce and my father's new marriage she was instructed to accept her new daughter-in-law's children as her grandchildren and to stay away from my mother. Regretfully, for her and my mother, this hurt them both as they were close. Ultimately it trickled down to my sister and I and the distance between her and us grew. My mother would speak to this and how my grandmother really didn't care for us. This, my mother's words, and Moo's gradual withdrawal from us, was mingled with our witnessing of her carrying this out. My sister and I would begin to spend time with my father and his new wife, and her children. And at times my grandmother was there as well. I could see how my step sisters were getting close to her and she close to them. For me, it cut like a knife and added another layer of feeling like I was defective in some way.

My mother became pretty bitter in a short time, downright nasty and angry. Maybe rightly so on some levels. It would be years after the divorce that I found out more of the circumstances surrounding the depth of my parent's division. As my mother's own need to retaliate with her number one weapon, my sister and I, against my father and his new family, we were held back at times from seeing any of them. Typically very trivial reasons and not really plausible. Thereby creating more distance.

Christmas was never the same, I've shared that. We were forbidden from seeing my father's side of the family most Christmases. Moo would stop by and drop our gifts off after the holiday and would never come into our house when she visited. Just a quick drop and run which was of course criticized by my mother. As I grew older the benefit of clarity, a renewed relationship, and all that was revealed, gave this all a new prospective.

Later in life she moved to Connecticut from Rhode Island and I'll never forget the day she left. My wife and I drove her to my uncle's place. Moo's go to color when dressing was black. Always with the heels to match. When she passed away she was cremated and it fell on my uncle's shoulders, my father's brother, to create a service for her. It was packed and in my uncle's theatrical fashion a black dress was displayed in her honor. She was a lively character and as I explained we had a commonality that bound us together.

She, like I, had a problem with the drink. As our relationship grew tighter and tighter as we both aged I tried with everything I had in me to help get her sober. (I did the same with Papa's sister who lived up at the pond who enjoyed hi-balls.) Eventually Moo did sober up. I don't think she had much of a choice after she moved. I would find her in the craziest situations and all I could do at times was watch with powerlessness.

My favorite was rousing her from her own lethargy and getting her on her feet. All I could do was carry her out of her place and into my apartment that I shared with my first wife. The look on my ex-wife's face when she arrived home was priceless.

She asked, "Um, what is Moo doing on the couch?" Moo was passed out.

To which I replied, "She's detoxing." Like this was a normal everyday occurrence.

Her disgust was evident and I think she left our apartment for the night. That was a part of the straw that broke the camel's back in my first marriage.

There are two other family members I've yet to mention or touch upon thus far. This would be my father's brother who became in all essence my father along with Papa. Papa would make a statement one day that was a direct hit.

"Thank God those kids have their uncle."

The other would be my father's sister. In my eyes she is "Super Mom." A truly dedicated one. It would be during one of the darkest and most uncertain times in my life that she would come forward and stiffen my backbone and resolve as a soon-to-be ex-husband and soon-to-be single father of my daughter.

I've tried to carefully lay out how those guiding forces were set in motion by what was handed to me. I tried to do this without causing pain to any family members who might be here yet I wish to remind you, and them, that this is a glimpse into what I perceived then, and now. There was so much more that could have been revealed, and may be, yet I do believe that my wife's own reaction to the writing as she reads it through shows me that I am hitting the necessary marks. And besides, you have your own life experiences that can be weaved into this. And hopefully you can relate to and indentify with some or all of this.

PART TWO

FEAR OF GOD

9- SLAPPING GOD

I've given you a meager glimpse into my childhood so far. There was so much more to it but I think this look back has lent some kind of basic idea of how my initial separation from God came to be. I also believe it's enough to make clear points for many of you to relate to on many planes even if our individual circumstances had different settings and flavors. It's the ultimate result of all of this, my *reaction,* that I really wish to get into.

All that I have divulged so far was very real for me as it was happening. I felt it through and through, to my core. My effort was to try and escape it all. I became an evader of reality which set up delusions on many fronts within my mind. I became a storyteller, to you, and to myself. I began to fasten a mask over my face and over my emotions. A mask that did not serve me well for nearly four decades. I didn't know this happened until years later.

Everything that I've shared so far happened over a period of a few short years. That's all it took to solidify that break away from God and set the foundation for the next few years as I clumsily trudged through life up to the day I found alcohol. And when that happened it was preceded by the first joint I smoked.

Maybe it's best to piece in a broad and overall look at my character up until the time I drank and weave in some experiences to give you an appreciation of the bearing my life took as well as the outlook I possessed.

This lesson about myself, the understanding of the result, did not come to me until I was forty-four years old. Today I am forty-nine. Plainly I could see the reality about me, I was living it, yet couldn't even venture a glimpse as to what the result those easily picked up ideas, emotions, and attitudes was. I could however see the guiding forces as I was living them daily. It was like I came up with new tricks over and over as I learned to cope with reality.

The deepest cut was the affect on my mind.

I was an honor roll student through elementary school and with the exception of changing another classmate's name on his assignment that one time I really didn't need to cheat to be an "A" student. I could perform but that would become more and more difficult as I became a person who needed to be the center of attention. The class clown always positioned me perfectly to rest at this spot.

I moved through elementary school with one recurring question at the forefront of my mind. "Where do I fit in and what is my role supposed to be?" I didn't know what my role was in the family until I started to get in trouble and once that began and I started to get some attention for it that role seemed to fit perfectly. I became the "black sheep" in the family. I didn't know what that meant but someone must have thrown that title on me at some point. My attitude was if the shoe fits, wear it. What was it that Papa taught me? If you're going to do something, do it right. I nailed that bitch down pretty hard through my life with my family. And I suppose I will always wear that label, even if only loosely, for the rest of my days. Ever watch the series "Sons of Anarchy?" There was a character that would answer everything with "I accept that." It was so with me. I accepted it.

I felt as though I never fit in and never knew what I was supposed to be. And this lasted well into my adult years. I would look at others and I could see how their own confidence cemented their positions and choices in life. I was without confidence. I was just lost and disoriented, I felt invisible to everyone around me.

I grew to a place where I really wanted to be accepted and loved but didn't want you to accept or love me. I was afraid to let you know what was really happening in my mind. I wanted to be successful in every area of my life yet was afraid to enjoy any success, I was fearful it would be taken away or would be short-lived. I wanted intimacy but didn't want anyone to get too close to me. I wanted to be at the top of everything I did yet was afraid of the applause. I wanted to give up daily and just stop the madness in my mind yet was afraid to, fearful that if I gave up I would lose whatever identity I thought I had. I wanted to be the center of attention but didn't want you to see me, I was afraid you might catch a glimpse of what was underneath the mask. I didn't care what you thought of me yet I so wanted your approval, and love. Basically I was fucked.

The greatest attributes to living a life disconnected from God are selfishness and self-centeredness. I would come to understand that these made up the root of all the troubles in my life. It would be years before I would come to understand that this disconnectedness, coupled with those attributes, led to a life of self-propulsion. And that in the end each and every trouble I experienced before I started with the drinking, while I was drinking, and all of the years that I spent in recovery, including my days now and those that lie ahead, were, are and will be of my own making. I did, have, and will cause them through my own perception.

So I became a liar, a cheat and a thief before the age of seven years old. I used to tell my wife "I was brought up to be a cat burglar." And over time and with practice I learned to perfect these shortcomings. As I grew more and more skilled with this way of living, being, I grew more and more anxious and apprehensive, more and more agitated and unsettled, more and more fractious and petulant, more and more envious and unhappy. I was never satisfied. My heart dimmed to a darkness that would allow no space or light for love, tolerance, kindness or patience. Unless of course there was something in it for me. And if there was something in it for me, or I thought there may be, I would pull one of my masks from my back pocket and slap it on my face for you. Even today, when I lose sight of God for but a moment that restlessness, irritability and discontentment returns from the recesses of my mind, and heart, and speaks to me. Admonishing me against the virtue of seeking God. I now know this is a trick of the ego, that lower self, looking for something to chew on to survive within me. Even at this moment as I type and share with you the voice of that nasty fuck, my ego, tries to speak to me.

"Really? You're writing a book? You? What do you have to offer anyone? You really think you will pull this off? Do you think or believe that your words will carry any weight in this world?" I have found that my ego prefers the negative side of things for nourishment.

Yet like resentments may be mastered so too can an exercise of power over that darkness within. I've learned It has to be something bigger than me. I had to find God.

As my life became more and more imperfect I demanded more and more perfection. No, not from me, from you. As my heart became darker my perception did as well. The farther and farther I distanced myself from God the more depth was added to my defects of character, my flaws. And I resented God more and more for not allowing me, as a human, the ability to manage my life effectively.

I remember a moment at Nana and Papa's house when it was only Nana and I together. We were talking in the dining room. I always felt safe asking her questions. We were speaking about God and prayer and I had a pit in my stomach that I couldn't define. Nana was the most pious person in the family. She had trinkets all over the place. If you opened the silverware drawer you might find a pair of praying hands. There's some irony, eh?

"Nana, where is God?"

"He is everywhere." Her response was as automatic as the vision of the rising sun on a clear morning.

I have always pushed the envelope as far as I could even from a young age. And this was one of those instances.

"Soooo...if I wave my hand through the air like this (with the motion of my hand to demonstrate) am I slapping God?"

She didn't answer this question. She just looked at me.

Have you ever wanted to go back in time and change something you have done or said or even change something that another did or said? This was one of those moments. Even to this day I wish I didn't ask that question. The look on her face was one of disappointment. I wish she had just grabbed me and held me. I wish she had shared with me what I'm about to share with you. The discovery I made after that spiritual upheaval I had that lasted for ninety days or so.

10 - FROM WITHIN AND SO WITHOUT

From the moment that first fear rose within with a light rumble like that of the beginning of a thunderstorm and brought with it that appendage, resentment, toward God, the channel between my spirit within to His Grace began to close. As I learned to hate and distrust this God, who I came to believe was out to get me, it's been a game of hide and seek. Each resentment I would encounter in life quickly became a substitute for my belief in God and His Power. And each of these resentments would compound one another. They led to even more resentments and even more division between my spirit and God. The channel, the avenue I believe He keeps open for us when He shoots us down here into physical form, became jammed up with the traffic of resentments and on the backside of these, fear followed close behind once the connection was broken.

For years I believed life here in my meatsuit was a cruel trick of His. Like He had this super huge table game set before Him and we were the pieces He played. Played with for His personal enjoyment and I grew to believe I had that same right and privilege. That life was some sort of twisted game and that I had to learn how to play it, and play it well.

Today I know that we are all here as spirits. This I always recognized. I suppose I've never believed in one life lived and then poof, it's over. We just happen to be wearing different suits, I call them meatsuits, and we all have different roles to play. With different purposes. For His Grace.

From the moment I looked upward and figuratively gave God the finger, screaming in my mind, "I'm all set with you; I'll do it on my own" I set out to prove I could play His game and be just as good at it. I thought I could wear His shirt. I had a friend years ago named "Big Ed" who saw this position I was trying to maintain and in casual conversation as I was complaining about all of the injustices in my life he offered this simple comment.

"Take the God shirt off, it doesn't fit you. It never will. And you look like an idiot trying to wear it." An omen of sorts.

The more I tried to play God the more I would see examples of His miracles. The force of nature being the most blatant. Could I produce a sunrise or sunset or the cycle the moon seems to enjoy on a monthly basis? Could I summon the tulip and hyacinth to bolt out of the ground in the spring? Could I paint the skies in the coolest shades of blue and on occasion change that painting by adding clouds to it? Could I blanket the green grass with rain or when the grass went to sleep in the winter tuck it in with a silent blanket of snow? Could I curl the water at the shore into the shape of a sideways cone and roll it onto the fine sands? Could I take a piece of glass and use my own powers to erode its edges and make it into a beautiful piece of sea glass and then redeposit it back onto the shore?

The answer to these questions is an authoritative "No!"

I tried to block out these questions, these ruminations, about my failure in playing God by trying with serious effort to focus on the "ugly trees." There was no profit in this battle as I couldn't deny the beauty around me. I couldn't evade His splendor, His triumph. Through my failure in playing God and noting these miracles I was coerced to ask "Who has this power?"

And deep within my being I would hear that voice that speaks to each of us, sometimes with a boom, "I did." It was God's voice speaking clearly through that spirit within, my intuition.

The more this channel that I was shot into this world with, an installed intuition, a sixth sense, became jammed up with resentments and fears the more I could only see the ugly trees. The resentments would sentence me to living in the past and the fears would keep me off center by depositing my mind in the future. This is not only true for alcoholics. This is the human condition. We all share it at some level. Some are able to rise above it, recognize it and get back to a place of neutrality, a center. Unfortunately many cannot. It was only when the channel became impossible to see through that I was able to submit to some form of surrender of my corrupted self-will.

I lost my Center.

I tried with whatever power I had within to clear this channel but to no avail.

I searched high and low for a solution to this

problem eventually finding it but it would be many painful years before that happened.

I read books. And then more books. Spiritual books, self-help books, religious books, books that would help me evade reality and serve as an escape only to return to this quandary of inexplicable circumstances. Music would provide a reprieve for a bit of time. But in time even my choice of music landed on flavors with dark lyrics.

The problem was that I was looking outside of myself for a solution. I was looking for a substitute for God. Wine, women, song, money, things. Not one of these would suffice or satisfy a deep yearning I had within to be repaired. Yet I refused to go back to God. The resentment I had toward Him had festered to the point of not being able to *recognize* the fact that if He had the Power over the laws of nature, proven laws over the material world, that perhaps He could be a Director for me. Aren't we, as humans, just as much a part of this physical world as that tulip or hyacinth flower? Those blue skies? Those clouds? The grass and rains and even the snow? The piece of glass? And if God can transform the glass, or anything He chooses to or is asked to, why shouldn't this apply to us as well? Why can't we be redeposited, redelivered, reinstalled?

After what was to happen through His Grace, a transformation that would never allow me to deny Him again, it was deep within that I did find Him.

11 - INTERMEZZO NUMBER FOUR

It is no secret at this point that I was able to break free from all that limited me to a three-dimensional world and was able to add another dimension to my life. But I did not wake up one day and think "Hey, I think I'll have a spiritual experience this year." Remember, my thinking was as corrupted as a computer with a virus and that blue screen of death would keep showing up daily for a long period of time. And I just kept trying to force my mind to reboot. Especially through distraction.

I once heard a friend share the following.

"My mind would have killed me a long time ago but it needed my body to get around."

I've had the fortune of being exposed to those twelve steps since I got sober at eighteen. I've told you this already. You may have some fixed ideas about AA and perhaps the people in AA. I get that, I really do. (I've got a few of my own.) They don't call it "Well People Anonymous." And for good reason; look at my story thus far. I only ask that you lay aside any prejudices or ideas you have about that for a time while I carry on with the story.

If one can look squarely at the body of the twelve steps or better yet *fully experience them* by thoroughly following their direction there is a result that is guaranteed. That result was initially described as a "spiritual experience" in the twelfth step when the first edition of their initial writing was published. It was later changed to "spiritual awakening." An awakening, or reawakening, of the spirit within. A reconnection to God.

There is a telling part in one of the chapters where an interaction between a man who never was a fellow of Alcoholics Anonymous sought help from Dr. Carl Jung. I won't bore you with the history surrounding this encounter yet I wish to use what the doctor described as a "spiritual experience" to deepen an appreciation of what exactly happened to me as my own experience through that set of principles produced this identical "description."

Dr. Jung described a spiritual experience in this way.

"They appear to be in the nature of huge emotional displacements and rearrangements. Ideas, emotions, and attitudes which were once the guiding forces of the lives of these men are suddenly cast to one side, and a completely new set of conceptions and motives begin to dominate them."[1]

Read it again if you must to fully appreciate what he was really saying.

I touched on the idea that if one is indeed a *real alcoholic* that they have placed themselves in a position of being *beyond human aid*. There are many that are not

---

[1] See Bibliography

alcoholics that may find themselves in this position. What exactly does this mean? At its fundamental level I'm led to understand that not one person can produce the spiritual experience, or awakening, in me. Nor can I do produce it in another person. I used the word produce in there. Yes, you might be able to act as a guide for someone as I had a guide walk with me and I may be able to do the same for others as was done for me, as you will see when we get to that part of the journey. But I can't *produce* it in someone. If I am indeed beyond human aid where am I to turn? Who can produce this essential psychic change so that I may recover this connection and add another dimension to my life?

God.

What the doctor offered this man decades ago in the way of an answer as to what had to happen if he wished to be free, and free from alcohol, is a tall order. You can't just walk into a doctor's office or a therapist's office and ask for a spiritual experience. If it was that easy I think there would be a line out the door of those seeking release and relief.

If I wished to be free from not only alcohol but those resentments and fears, the guilt, shame and remorse from a life lived selfishly and in a self-centered style this is what I would have to experience. This would be the only way to clear that channel. It was well after I had a spiritual upheaval and started the research of what the hell just happened to me that brought me back to this interaction and the doctor's description. I was amazed at how his description was spot on for me. It was eerie, considering those words were published decades ago.

I had to have all of the emotions I carried

through life since giving God the finger *displaced*. They had to be *rearranged*. My *attitude* toward them had to be rearranged, my perspective. The ideas, emotions, and attitudes had to be fully examined with a fine-toothed comb in an effort to see how they formed those guiding forces that were set up. I had to muster the willingness to let them go, the willingness to try something different. I had to see the futility, the uselessness, of those ideas, emotions, and attitudes. and further the ineffectiveness of the resultant guiding forces. Once I was successful at getting a full and deep appreciation of the futility, then, and only then, did my willingness match God's favor in having them cast aside. I had to be absolutely, unquestionably, no ifs, ands, or buts, leveled. I had to be broken down.

I had to muscle my way through that dark night of the soul. And it wasn't pretty or comfortable. Quite the contrary. But when you're dry firing a pistol into your mouth to practice an exit from reality is there another alternative? (I did try one other alternative before this happened but that part of the story is for later on as well.)

For me, there was not.

I had to walk a path that many cannot endure. And then maintain what I had found. Again something many cannot do.

And then I would have to share this experience with others as a shift in my relationship with God dictates. I shifted from a concentration on the self to a concentration and focus on what He would have me be. I had to become an agent for Him and begin living a spiritual life. This is not always easy.

Do you recall when I shared about travelling to

my father and step mother's home to come clean? I intentionally left something out of that story as I needed it to land here for you.

There were many things said and asked of me by my step mother during this meeting. In the midst of this meeting there must have been some recognition on her part that something had changed, had shifted in me. She wasn't speaking to the person she knew throughout the years. She revealed this to me with a couple of questions.

She ventured, "Did you join a church?"

As I considered where she was going I answered, "No. I didn't."

The next one, "Are you born again?"

What I answered then would not match the answer I would reply with today.

"No, it's not like that."

I answered that question from a perspective reached out of the first question yet in reality this is *exactly* what happened to me. I was born again.

Now I don't know much about religion and will admit I'm a "holiday Catholic." If the nudge is there during the holidays I'll make my way to church for a mass. I do appreciate the church setting and the way one's focus is concentrated on God while in a cloud of frankincense. I can recite the "Our Father" and can fully appreciate the selfless connotation put forth in that prayer yet I can't recite the "Hail Mary" and can admit I do not know all of the required replies during a mass. I often find myself mumbling them or just moving my lips.

In many respects the description Dr. Jung offered is a form of being born again. I had to be willing to let the old self die and endured the pain of watching him slowly wither away over the course of two years. And then I was able to enjoy a re-birth as a new set of ideas and conceptions began to form and take hold within. A new design. Ideas and conceptions that began to establish a fresh set of motives...guiding forces. That was equally as painful. I don't know if that pain matched the physical pain a woman endures while giving birth but it certainly lasted a lot longer. I came to know death and rebirth as a necessary period of time in what I would call a trip into the "garden of good and evil." Half of which is dark, dirty and dangerous with the other being vividly brilliant in color, crisp and clean, and safe.

12 - SETTLING FOR LESS AND THE DAY TRUTH BECAME DANGEROUS

Now these years between the explosion in the family and the first time I smoked a joint are loaded with memories yet they are jumbled with respect to their place in any form of timeline in my life. If I jump all over as I cover these years please bear with me. It's their point that will be of use to the story.

A natural by-product of the violent emotional tornado I was living was the ability to become that chameleon. My mask grew different looks over the years based on the people around me, the job I was working, or the family member I was with at any given moment. Along with the lies. I would burn up energy with the effort of trying to remember and keep the lies straight. This coupled with the number of denials I would have to keep at the ready in the event a question or accusation was floated in my direction brought me to place of learning how to settle for less.

At the end of my time in elementary school, the sixth grade, it already began, that settling for less. I turned twelve before the end of the school year and tried with all of my might to keep muscling through

ROBERT ERNEST BACH

by seeking attention wherever I could. Both good and bad.

Somewhere in the midst of these years I began an effort to be and place first in all that I did. In many instances I succeeded and in others I failed. The thing with me is that for some reason everything seemed to have a crazily-deep bearing on my being. Right to my core.

Successes became a drug, I got high off of them. And failures sent me into a spiral of depression and sadness.

I was actually a great student and great grades came naturally to me, without much effort. I had a great fifth grade teacher in school and she recognized that I could really spell. She encouraged me to start entering spelling bees. I did and excelled. I recall when we went to another school and watched a bee in preparation for one I would be in. As we stood together against a wall one of the contestants was asked to spell "vacuum." She turned to me before the student could spell it and asked me to spell it. V-a-c-u-u-m. Piece of cake. She smiled. And you know I loved that shit!

As I worked my way to the stage of the local junior high school and participated in a larger contest I made it to the end with only one word to nail for the win. Needless to say I missed it and I'll never, ever, ever, ever spell "aggressive" wrong again until the day I die.

I spiraled downward from there. A big piece of me just gave up at a deeper level.

During this time the reward I was seeking for any win or gain in that arena was clean. That is to say without motive. This would be my final year in this school as it was closing and I would be finishing my final year in the elementary grades in a different school.

Now fast forward a bit to the next year. New school. New students. New people to impress. I had two teachers in this school and one of them a man named Mr. Coppolelli. Each Friday he had us stand around the perimeter of the classroom for his spelling bee. The prize was a crisp one dollar bill. Yes, I killed it practically every week. But something was different as those guiding forces matured almost of their own accord, like something else was inside me now. That something was my motive for winning. I was there to impress and was reaching an age when sex was becoming the predominant thought in my mind. I was already waking up with a hard on every morning. But I wasn't measuring it yet.

The key factor I wish to put across here is that my ability to excel was now wrapped in a motive and the motive was based in self-centeredness. It went from just casual sport to a level of nourishment for that self-centeredness that always seemed to massage my growing and faulty ego.

I moved from that place of doing something and doing it right with gusto to only doing something if there was something in it for me. I began to settle for less. By the time I left that school and sixth grade I had already tossed my hands up and took on the air of "What's the fucking use?" It was the last year that my name would grace an honor roll and a few weeks before I smoked my first joint.

I now recognize that each of the failures I experienced, whether scholastically, in relationships, emotionally, mentally, physically, financially or (fill in the blank) were actually calling cards. They were calls from God. They were a call away from my own failure in power to His Power. I chose to ignore them. At times I had an occasional thought along the plane of "I can't do this by myself anymore." But perception, clogged up with ugly trees, resentments and fears, and now a miniscule consciousness of the harms I was causing others at times had its own power over me. Perception had a real hold on me.

The day arrived when the nail in the coffin that carried the idea of speaking the truth was hammered home. Speaking the truth would become a fear.

My mother was pretty pissed off with and battered by life. She set out to piss off my father in any way she could as often as she could whenever she could, and naturally his new wife too.

My sister and I came home from school one day and my mother was sitting in the living room with a look on her face that can only be described as solemn. We were told to sit down and that she wanted to read something to us. A letter had arrived in the mail. It was addressed to her and it was from my step mother. It was after this letter was read aloud that I began to refer to my step mother as my step monster.

The letter was as explosive as the dynamite that blew us all apart years before. Explosive in truth. My step mother called my mother out on everything she put her and my father through in just a few short years. I do not need to elaborate on its content here. Just know it hit every mark that each missile was targeted on. And she even managed to throw the imperfections of my sister and I in there for great measure. As my mother read it aloud I began to feel extremely uncomfortable. More uncomfortable than my father looked when my step mother was holding my feet to the fire years later. I don't think my mother saw this in me and I can't recall my sister's reaction to this. My sister and I never spoke about it after this day. I don't remember the rest of this day or night. Another blackout of sorts.

My mother cried as she read it. In later years when she and I spoke about it she explained that all of the accurate truths, accusations, were painful for her and ripped apart every fiber of her being. When my mother finally finished reading it she prefaced her one question to us with a pleading of her case and innocence.

"Is it true?," She wanted to be convinced otherwise.

I know I said that it wasn't and do believe my sister did as well. For a short time we, my sister and I, attempted to prop my mother up and bolster her sense of worth in this world. Yet to no avail. She simply gave up after that. She was never the same.

From this gem of an experience I learned to write my own "letters" seeking to destroy and retaliate in kind. The effect has been the same, a near-destruction of the relationship between I and the recipient of my words.

ROBERT ERNEST BACH

13 - GOD WAS ALWAYS THERE

Before we take leave of the place in my journey that was designed to give you a glimpse of my time in that pinball machine I would feel as though I neglected an area of importance if I didn't address this. It did take me years and years to understand what beyond human aid meant and the implication of it. Or the flip side of the coin, living a life by self propulsion only.

Nana was a rock for me. Solid not only in her confidence but in her faith.

Papa was a rock for me. Also solid in his confidence. And principles.

And then there was my uncle, my father's brother. The number of years between he and my father and then he and I is near equal. He was older than I and already had a grasp on adulthood yet young enough to be able to easily relate to me. He was merciful with me until I pissed him off too.

He became my father by substitution and just by the mere fact that he was present. He was there for my sister and I. He became my older brother as a consequence of his age and ability to reach me at times when so many others could not. He was my cool uncle who would eventually share a smoke of a joint with me. He was a teacher in many respects and it was easy for me to ask questions as a student in this world. He eventually moved to the next state over and his absence was felt but added a level of excitement to my day when I knew he would be visiting. And at times his lessons served as teachings in trying new things.

He would invite me to his home the next state over and arrangements were made for me to get on a Greyhound bus and travel the distance alone. He encouraged this when I was young, before I began the drugs and drinking.

He became a rock in my life as well.

As much as I tried to evade and ignore God, His signs, His omens, I could recognize at some level the depth of appreciation that my uncle and Nana had for God. It's just that my thinking ran along the train of "I'm glad you feel that way. I'm glad you have that but He doesn't give a shit about me."

It would be these three "rocks" that would create a dependence on people for my happiness and peace. I sought them instead of God. I didn't have any resentments against them that might serve as roadblocks to trust.

Over the years there have been a few others in my life that became those rocks. I was always looking for a substitute for the Real Thing. As though if I kept my mind's eye on these *stronger* people, my *grounding* in them, I would somehow one day be able to take this position in life. I suppose that the reason these family members appealed to this sense is because they provided a level of comfort to me. They protected me from all of those obnoxious bumpers in the pinball machine whenever it was in their own power to do so.

Nana spoke to God's Grace and lived a life of demonstration with this Undercurrent that always flowed below her surface.

Papa didn't speak to God's Grace but his own demonstration was evident in his own actions and when he made recognition of Him as the Grand Architect.

My uncle spoke to God's Grace very openly with me, even when we were smoking a joint. As a gay man who came out in a time when it required an overwhelming amount of courage to do so and to still believe in God was easily visible to me. I'll never forget the look on my mother's face when I returned home from a weekend at he and his partner's home and prodded my mother to know why the two of them shared the same bedroom.

I really wanted to, deep within, believe in God. And the closest I could get was by creating substitutes. I had to use the faith of those around me to recognize God. I now appreciate that it was always my spirit within that yearned to be reconnected to its Maker. The number one resentment always got in the way and this was a battle that raged within me most of my life. It became a war of self-will versus God's will. And I always erroneously believed that my will was the victor of these battles.

God's always won when all was said and done.

As we make our way out of part two and begin part three where I begin to share about the first drink and the brief six years before it cut me down it might be wise to let you in on something, a clarification for you. The impression you may be getting is that I hold everyone in my life in contempt for what happened to me. I did, and for a long time. I do not today. You may have also gotten the impression that compared to the cast of characters in my life, those discussed and even those who may appear in later pages, I'm portraying myself as perfection personified. Nothing could be further from the truth than this. As a matter of fact I tempered the first two parts of this writing and could have added ten more pages to each chapter if I wanted to present this from a victim's viewpoint. That would serve no purpose for you, for me or for God.

It's easy to write about others, their successes and failures. I know many who can tackle that task easily. The most difficult part of my writing will be the second part of that adage that goes something like this. When you point the finger at another turn your hand over and take note of the three fingers pointing back at you. It has always been this way with me. What I have seen and see in others, I am or have been in my thoughts, and life.

I am not a perfect husband or father, son or brother, nephew or cousin, friend or associate, employer or employee. I've yet to come across a meatsuit, a spirit wrapped in a physical body, who is.

I've hurt a great many people with a life lived by self-propulsion, before I started the drinking, while drinking, and ironically more so as I got clean and sober and stayed sober. And even after I had a spiritual upheaval that changed my perception and personality, I still hurt people. And even today, when a disconnect between God and I becomes operative, I will hurt people.

I have put my wife through hell. My children have never seen me drink yet the effects of my own spiritual deficiencies have had their affect on them. Through seeming retaliation and even as a result of the character flaws that grew in me I've hurt my parents deeply and pretty much was a great part in destroying the relationship with my sister and step sisters. I'm self-employed and it's a rare day when I'm perfect with myself. I believe we are all on the same journey, back to our Maker, and there will be times of discomfort yet there *can be* mostly peace, peace of mind and peace in our hearts, and most importantly peace in spirit.

ROBERT ERNEST BACH

PART THREE

I TOOK THE DRINK AND THE DRINK TOOK ME

14 - "HI NEIGHBOR! HAVE A 'GANSETT"

For the purpose of my story I will use the word alcohol. Know that this includes all of the other crap I jammed into my physical body to medicate my mind and spirit. It will be easier to use that one word "sober" to describe the near-identical phrase "clean and sober." When I use the word "drunk" it will serve to encompass the words "high" or "lit" or "blasted" or whatever your experience might be or might have been. I'm not here to debate the difference between an alcoholic and a drug addict, I consider myself to be both and for me they, and the recovery, are one and the same.

If you are young I encourage you to keep

reading. If you are older, the same. If by chance you are having difficulty with the drink yourself I would encourage you to keep reading on and perhaps you might be able to relate to a bit of my story. If you are involved with or married to someone with a problem with alcohol, read on. This is one area where I hope I am of use to you, and ultimately God. This is where I hope you get a clearer understanding of an often wildly misunderstood illness this is.

When I started drinking I was already a daily smoker, Marlboros thank you very much. Hell I had been smoking Chesterfields for most of my life while at my grandparent's house or Kools while trapped in my father's car with the air conditioner on as a bystander. Smoking cigarettes came naturally. As natural as the drink did.

I drank alcohol, and did as many drugs as I possibly could, for a period of six years. I was twelve when I started and eighteen when I was able to get clean and sober and break free from the physical compulsion and mental obsession I had acquired. Those two elements that make me an alcoholic were acquired in a short period of time. I would venture to say within the very first year that I started.

I had tried alcohol at times before the age of twelve, a sip here and a sip there yet I had no immediate fascination with it. Perhaps the spiritual sickness wasn't in the perfect position to see it as a solution, yet. My neighborhood grew up on Narragansett beer and Ballantine Ale, readily-available to all of us kids through our families and a foreman at the local brewery who lived across the street, and whatever other spirits we could get our hands on from our parents. Or by using that power of persuasion on the older kids willing to get it for us from the liquor store.

Over the period of six years I did an equal amount of drugs as I would the drink. I always seemed to prefer drugs as they always brought me to places that were unpredictable. I loved trippy drugs and the farther I went with these the farther I knew I could go. There was always something more powerful out there to pull me away from reality, the pinball machine.

My first real experience involved pot. I smoked a joint with a couple of guys I became fast friends with after I left the sixth grade. There was some peer pressure involved, isn't there typically? We went into the woods. Two guys with experience and one naive one. When we left the woods three experienced guys emerged. I fucking loved it! I mean really, really fucking loved it!

And from that moment the chase was on. The effect was that superb for me! And I would, for the next six years, be chasing that initial effect. Hence the escalation of the use and abuse and proclivity to seek other substances or varieties of alcohol to capture that very first experience.

If I could place a grade on one summer during my adolescent years that ranked the highest it would be this one. The first summer as a teenager and the one that saw the only enjoyment in my drinking. They progressively went downhill as each year passed. Eventually leading to the downhill turn each month took. And then each day. And then each hour. And then each moment. I was never able to capture the splendor of that first time again. The progression of this illness was that fast for me.

It all started innocently. I said at the very start of the book that I didn't set out to be an alcoholic. It wasn't a goal. I didn't wake up one day after leaving the sixth grade and have a thought like "Maybe today I'll start on becoming an alcoholic." I've yet to meet one man or woman who made a fully-conscious decision to do so. I did however make that decision to turn my back on God, thereby creating the fertile ground for alcohol to have its way with me. I had that underlying cause of alcoholism, that spiritual sickness, long before I began drinking. The drink seemed to be the perfect *solution* for it.

So where does this really fit into the equation of everything we have spoken about so far? Those ideas? Those emotions? And those attitudes? Those guiding forces? The motives? And the conceptions? The finger I gave God? That spiritual sickness deeply settled within me that neither I nor anyone could recognize or pick up on?

That answer is the simplest part of an equation that would seem to land at a sum called a solution. And I will try my damnedest to keep the answer to my own experience and free of opinions.

Like most sicknesses that need to be *treated*, mine most definitely did. That spiritual sickness needed a treatment to create relief and release from it. I have spent every moment of my life since that first resentment toward God seeking that treatment, a solution. The key word in that last line is the word "I." I, me, myself. The egotistically spiritually sick person who made a decision to do it my way. I walked in a bewildered state for years searching and searching and at some points I believed, delusionally, without sound reasoning, that I had come upon it.

This is the combustion I felt throughout my being when introducing substances into my system that altered my state, my constitution. The relief I felt from anger, fear, restlessness, and discontent was electric. It was instant. And it worked fabulously. In the blink of an eye I felt free for the first time in years. I felt a part of. I felt as though I could now decide what I would like to be in life. I felt as though there was ease and like that freedom I felt for the first time in years I felt comfort. And of course this all turned into a great source of fuel for my ego, my pride. And to exacerbate that division between me and God I felt justified in telling Him to screw. I did this consciously by thinking "See? I told you I could make my way through life without you." He probably laughed and moved another piece on the game board settling to just wait it out for me to turn back to Him.

The thing for me, someone craving a solution to my problems, was that alcohol became a medication. It was an immediate remedy. At least it appeared to be. And it worked for a short time. In no time at all it began to cause problems in my life in every area. That short time was probably about a month or so.

In no time at all the use and abuse added another level of deceit, thievery, and cheating to my already honed repertoire of tricks. More colors to my chameleon mask I worked so hard on to keep in tip top shape. At this young age you really can't declare that you have begun drinking to solve your problems and besides the legal drinking age was still nine years away for me. So you lie and pin it on your friends when you're caught with booze. When you aren't really making any money to support the cost of this new medication, especially on paper route money, you begin to come up with created ways of "borrowing" money to get it, leading to the selling of dried goods and using, literally, the "profits." I quickly learned to cheat death with some of the crap I was doing.

I shared earlier on about what actually makes someone a *real alcoholic*. Those two components being the phenomenon of craving, that physical allergy, and the mental state while drinking but even more curious the state of thinking that an alcoholic possesses *before* one even picks up a drink. That *alcoholic mind*. Did I have these two elements from the very first hit or drink? I don't think it was there immediately, yet the cause of it all, the spiritual malady and deficiency was.

I don't remember the thinking I had the morning after this first experience but I'm confident that there was a feeling, or yearning, within, to repeat it. There had to be. In quick order I had these two components there, inside of me, an insidiousness that I never even saw. An insidiousness dwarfed by my elation at this newfound discovery that masqueraded as a solution. I wouldn't wake up to the fact that I had a problem with the drink for about six years as it became second nature to blame everyone around me for my own defects of character and drinking. I held everyone hostage with my contempt and their own shortcomings.

When I began drinking my life was still full with all of the people that were there when I was growing up with the exception of one. Nana. Nana had breast cancer and made a valiant effort in fighting it. I offer this to you through the benefit of hindsight. I never knew she was sick. I was never told about it. I don't know why, she never even told me.

There was this new spirit about her that I did take notice of however. She began knitting. Feverishly knitting. She knitted afghans and comforters like it was her responsibility to blanket every cold child with them. To this day the one I have from her, with every color of the rainbow in it, is never far from my reach. In fact I know that it's in the next room in a linen cabinet as I type. It has to be just about the warmest thing I've laid on my body, it's like she is woven into the yarn. I call it "Nana."

Her spirit moved her to make some changes around her and Papa's home. She was always getting things done as if life was a giant checklist waiting for items to be crossed off of it. The area rugs in the dining room and living room were replaced with wall to wall carpeting in a rose / orange / peach shade and there are times today when I'm designing flowers that I'm reminded of her when I use a variety of rose called "Cherry Brandy." The walls were all repapered and my favorite burgundy-colored linoleum floor in the kitchen was torn up and replaced with a new look.

She would shop weekly at the grocery store and they had that "Dish of the Week" thing going on where you could buy the piece or multiples for what amounted to be pennies. Poof. Multiple sets of dishes carefully packed away in the house. She bought canned goods like we were going back to war in the near future and would need them to survive a zombie apocalypse. Fruits and veggies in every size can you can imagine. Papa was legally blind at this point in his life and I think if he wasn't she would have bought a new vehicle as well.

She was getting ready to die and to me it was just that usual "can do" spirit she had. She was preparing all of us with what we would need after she was gone. I swear she knew Papa would never do these things that needed to be updated. I like to think that each of the creations she made out of yarn like a sweatshop worker while she suffered silently were left behind to remind us of her, and her legacy. This is the exact feeling evoked from my core when I blanket myself with her gift on a cold day or night.

I came home from school one day when I was in the sixth grade and Nana was at the house. It was the middle of the week and out of character with the flow of how things usually played out. When I saw her car in the driveway as I arrived home I became happy, naturally. I wasn't drinking yet. When I went into the house there was this peculiarity about the house. She and my mother were sitting side by side on the couch and I knew instinctively that I had interrupted a serious conversation by the looks on their faces. You could feel the gravity in the room and it wasn't the stale air that seemed to be locked within since the explosion.

Nana's attention quickly turned to me.

"How was school love?" The other nickname she had for me.

"It was good." I hesitated to add more as that instinct told me there was something coming from her and I had better pay attention to it.

Some more small talk and then this was extended to me.

"I hope you never smoke those marijuana cigarettes." With the most serious look I've ever seen on her face.

"I won't Nana." My reply, a lie, came from me automatically as I never wanted to disappoint her.

I knew something was amiss but quickly turned back into myself and dismissed it.

It was only a short time later that my sister and I were not awakened for school. We were allowed to sleep in. My mother wasn't home the previous night and I thought she was working late. She wasn't. She was at the hospital with Papa and when they arrived the doctors were trying to resuscitate my grandmother. She had a massive heart attack and died.

It fell on my mother's shoulders to tell us what happened when we finally woke up that morning. All I could do was cry. And cry. And cry. My rock, my own personal power greater than me was now gone. I felt so alone, and paralyzed, with fear. Naturally another layer of distaste, disgust and hate was added to my already misaligned perception of God. "You bastard" was all that I could think of Him. It became very convenient to blame Him for injustice and conversely it became easy to praise myself for the opposite.

Papa was not the same person after Nana died, nor were my mother and I. I was most certainly lost and all the more reason alcohol fit into the sum of all things labeled solution. Papa would say that he just wanted to "go too." My mother gave up at an even deeper level. Individually and collectively we were alone now. It turned out she was a rock for them as well. None of us ever spoke to this and this is what I see as I revisit this time in our lives with memory.

The battles between my mother and father continued on their normal heading through the storm. Like a "letter" was going to change anything?

It just added salt to the wounds. I was allowed to be at Nana's wake and funeral at that young age and I will always feel a deep gratitude for this decision that was made for me. At the wake I was allowed to stand "in the line" with my mother, Papa and my sister. It was now just the four of us. My father came to the service and paid his respects. There was this brief truce between my parents. Not the white flags of surrender, just a cordial and respectful truce.

I left the line and sat in the front row of chairs to look upon Nana as she lay there in her casket. My father came up from behind and sat with me for a bit. I have no idea what he said. There weren't any of the usual politics that typically accompanied my parent's war. This I recall. I guess it was that expected parental concern and consolation.

The following morning my uncle arrived to support us and it was arranged for him to drive his little MG convertible behind the limo my sister and I floated in. I remember looking out the back window in an effort to keep him in my sights. Deep inside I wanted to be *grounded*. As we left the church and made our way to the cemetery for the last part of the service he broke from the line of cars and took a turn away from us. He had to get back to his stream of life. He waved and made funny faces and all I could summon from my body was a weak wave.

It would be a day or so before I paid for breaking away from that line and sitting in the front row to just observe Nana in her box. My mother chastised me for speaking with my father at the wake. The war was back on again and I guess this was the way my mother gave the order that I was being reenlisted.

Papa lived for many years after and I swear he

stuck around to do the exact same thing Nana did for him and for us. He wanted to make sure that we were all set and taken care of. I'll write about that and the effect it had on me when we reach that part of the spiritual journey.

I began junior high school, seventh grade, at this same time. I did like junior high. New faces, larger classes, and different teachers throughout the day. And now I had Nana's passing to use to my advantage when I got in trouble. Same gig as when I was in the second grade. A few tears and most times all was forgiven or looked over.

Of course with one of my higher powers gone now I would need another one to put in its place. I lost my virginity that first year in junior high school and like the drink I would chase sex now too. Not in the manner that some use it, like the alcoholic uses the booze, but on a different plane. I was quick to associate sex with love and admiration and I would carry this *idea* around until I met my wife of today.

I continued the use and abuse of alcohol and as I did my physical tolerance for it grew. It took more and more to gain some kind of effect from it. Eventually I started to lose pieces from my recollection of what happened when I drank. At first there were moments of grey outs. Not total blackouts. Just bits and pieces of what I had been doing and saying were fuzzy or lost. These grew in frequency and did eventually lead to blackout drinking. I would lose bigger and bigger chunks of time. I would wake up in different places and not recall how I got there. I have a friend who calls it "time travelling" when he is being witty.

The effect of starting to settle for less, coupled with the drinking and my not really giving a shit about anything affected my grades. As I said there was to be no more honor roll for me. And when Nana died any care I had left in the tank for grades evaporated instantly. I could always perform in school with zero effort and managed to lumber my way through junior high school with "C's" and an occasional "B."

I became one of those problem students for my teachers and the administrators, especially the vice principal. I visited his office frequently and after school detention became my last class of the day. It became perfectly acceptable to me to be this kind of person. The more I drank the less I cared. About you, about my parents, my sister, school, the teachers and counselors who tried to reach me every day, and ultimately myself.

The idea of just checking out, dying, started before I entered high school.

I stopped caring. The idea of capturing that initial reaction of getting high faded as I started to accept at some level within that even that was now an impossibility. I think I knew I was fucked with the alcohol long before I was able to break free from it. It's just that direct consequences from its use didn't warrant any more than this fleeting thought. It wasn't bad enough yet. It wasn't causing any damage that *moved* me yet although it was having an effect on my mother and sister. I grew to be an absolute asshole in my mother's house.

This led to two simple words being screamed at me. Those same exact damn words I heard when I was seven years old and in second grade. The same explosive words that were screamed at my father.

Words that led to the changes in my life causing that first resentment born out of fear. And when these were screamed at me the winds of change blew just as violently in my life as they had seven years prior.

When I was fourteen years old I was in the last year of junior high school, the ninth grade, and there was a miniscule part of me looking forward to going to high school. Like I was a few steps closer to being an adult. Like there was some new freedom attached to that magical passage in life.

"Get out!"

"Magic to my ears. See ya!," Were the two thoughts I answered this with as I looked into my mother's eyes for the last time for what would be two years. My sister's and Papa's eyes as well.

ROBERT ERNEST BACH

15 - AND THEN SHE SCREAMED "GET OUT"

These were the words I had been waiting to hear for years. It's like they were expected and I was just waiting for them to be directed at me. I got out. I left the house and ran. I took flight like a bank robber on foot with the police in hot pursuit.

And for the first time in years I felt what my father may have felt. Freedom. The same freedom I could feel in his apartment when I was there at a young age. New beginnings are like that. Still are for me when a door closes in my life and a new one is opened. It's like going on vacation. Your senses are heightened. Ever notice that? The colors are more vivid, and brighter. The air smells and even seems fresher. Foods taste better. People are better looking and even music and words are filled with more melody. Yeah, it was like that. For about two months I think.

The inherent problem with a change of scenery as I experienced them in my life is that I always took myself with me. I couldn't let anything go and leave it behind and by now the drinking, the medicinal effect I was always seeking from the first time, was of zero use. The tolerance had grown too deep and it was now a habit. I had become an alcoholic and my father and step mother had no idea what they were about to get into with me. And what they would be exposing their daughters to.

I ran to my friend's house, the brother of the girl who solved the whole virginity problem I was having. I wasn't looking for solace from them. I just wanted to use their telephone to call my father. I called him and he said he would be right there. He asked where I was and I asked him to drive down a specific street, that when I saw him I would jump in his car. I was hiding on someone else's enclosed porch as I knew my mother knew exactly what was going to happen with those magical words. She knew I was going to get out.

As I hid on this stranger's porch with a puppy they had left there I sat on a chair and waited. When I sat down the chair collapsed on the puppy's leg and I think I broke his leg. There was no time to seek help for the puppy, my own selfishness and self-centeredness were on high alert and that would be an impossibility in that state. My needs outweighed the pain I caused the puppy. It would be like this when it came to people in my life for many years as well.

A sleek looking 280Z, a Datsun, dark grey in color and one I didn't recognize came flying down the street and something told me to jump off of the porch, that it was him. He took a friend's car to come and get me, he didn't want my mother to recognize or see his own vehicle in the neighborhood. My father left his business that day to come and retrieve me and would enter a battle with my mother that I never fully appreciated until this moment as I type these memories for you. Quite frankly, I had forgotten about that puppy up until now too.

We went to his house and he showed me around. I hadn't been there in years. He had a pool table downstairs and he taught me how to play that afternoon. When the state police arrived he told me to stay downstairs. Eventually they had to check my welfare or something like that and when they were satisfied that I was not in danger I was allowed to stay there. The age of fourteen was good enough to execute a decision, and besides they didn't have a warrant or order to take me back to my mother's house. It was a Friday; too late to get one.

Later in the evening my father's effortless coup of gaining one of his kids was celebrated by all of us, which included his wife and her three daughters. I slept on the couch downstairs and eventually after all of the legal crap was satisfied I was able to live there. The judge ruled I was old enough to decide.

I fell in quickly with everyone and became a part of. Something I always craved.

I didn't have the benefit of packing a bag when I left my mother's and left my clothes behind much like my father had left some of his stuff behind when he left years before. It was great to have all new clothes and a host of all new instant friends. It felt like a reboot of the computer again but in short time the insidiousness of my true disconnected-from-God character came to the surface. That blue screen of death would pop up again.

When I speak to alcohol as I lived with my father

know that it was pot and drugs. The drink was not accessible and smoking pot was acceptable to he and his wife. We all smoked pot. I did manage to wipe out their bottles above the refrigerator in the kitchen cabinet and I'm confident that all of those bottles were straight water when I left their house a short time later.

I was transferred from one school and enrolled in another and when it came to pick my classes, they let me pick them, the guidance counselor included, I chose classes that I had already taken. I had already taken Algebra I and in the new school I chose Algebra I again. And not only that, I opted for "Part One," an even lighter version. I was already in my third year of French and doing pretty good with it. I went back to the first year of French. This was the year that I began taking the easy way out. Of course this extended to everything in time and would last for a few decades.

I trudged along and used and abused alcohol and drugs, all the while growing more and more resentful. My father was closer to his step daughters and seemed to enjoy a camaraderie with them we never had. My step mother was the disciplinarian and I didn't care for that but most times the extent of punishment was the removal of the cue ball from the pool table.

I grew to have zero respect for their home even when they extended every opportunity to me for a great life that might have been laced with a great education. I had no appreciation in me for all that they tried to do for me.

The spiritual sickness buried with alcohol and its abuse creates this breeding ground for delusions in the mind. I did get a job in a restaurant as a dishwasher and a busser on the weekends. My friend and I worked there together and we had a blast while working. But like most everything else I had zero respect for anyone there either. I thought that my abilities were underrated. Like I should have been managing the joint and its affairs at the age of fifteen.

The waitresses would feed us drinks when we worked at night and we always convinced our parents to let us sleep outside in a tent on these nights. This made for some pretty drunk nights. And some crazy-ass bike rides home by way of a four lane highway. I don't know how we didn't get killed.

My father and step mother did everything in their own power to hand me a better life. I refused it. It was impossible to focus on the betterment of my own life. I was now under the madness of the drink. I was oblivious to this. And even when I was given a glimpse it was easily dismissed. It was during this time that I became an avid reader. My step mother handed me the book "Cujo" and I devoured it. Reading became an escape from reality.

I began my old tricks of stealing. My step mother tried to teach me how to manage money and required that I give her my cashed paycheck along with the paystub. She knew I was spending it on pot. On the backside of trying to teach me how to manage my money I think there was the belief on her part that she might gain some kind of sway over my habit. That she might somehow be able to temper it. I would sneak into their bedroom and search her desk for the envelope that contained my paystub and cash. I took some of the cash from it and when confronted about it I lied and told her it wasn't me. I was actually that delusional to think I was successful at pulling the wool over her eyes. Like I had somehow persuaded her that she was losing her mind while I was trying with all of my own limited power to hang onto mine. I was a hot mess. I certainly lived up to being that "black sheep."

My step sisters showed me where our parents hid their dope and when I failed to get some from another source I helped myself to my parents.

I'm confident that most teenagers wake each morning with a swirl of thoughts about the day. Adults too. Some are probably crisp and clean and filled with hope for a successful day. Some may have a sense of fear wrapped around them. Some may elicit a smile. Some anger. By this time in my journey my mind shifted to delusional thinking, believing every lie I told myself, and I could focus on resentments only. None of my thoughts were filled with hope, only despair. No love anywhere to be found in them. And now I had that fully established *alcoholic mind.* Upon wakening my thoughts went directly to the alcohol and drugs. I felt comfort if I knew I was covered for the day, a sense of relief as if this were the only problem or trouble in the world. (Well, in my world, my mind, it was.) If I didn't have this problem solved when I woke up, even after trying to solve the problem before passing out the night before, I would be gripped with a fear that added more layers of confused thought on top of the already confused, peculiar and perverted thinking that I had. If you are not an alcoholic you may not understand the gravity of this situation. If you are, either still drinking or sober, you might be nodding your head right now.

In this state of fear this was my thinking in the

morning when I came alive from being passed out most nights. And remember I had become a thief years before.

"Where am I going to get it?" Each self-imposed question would gain in volume and pressure.

"Who am I going to get it from?"

"How the fuck am I going to get it!?!"

And when there was no money?

"What can I steal and sell to get the money to get it?"

"How the fuck am I going to get through today!?!"

I would endure and live like this for two years. The most mentally brutal two years I've ever lived. Pot's not a gateway drug? It was for me.

The spiritual malady, the illness, led to full blown alcoholism in three short years. The sad part is that the first symptoms to present themselves born out of the spiritual disconnect were never seen or recognized by me or my family. We didn't know. And then the most pronounced and visible symptoms of that spiritual disconnect, the use and abuse of alcohol no matter what the cost, were not seen with equal ignorance. This is the mind fuck with alcoholism. The attendant denial born out of ignorance, the not knowing what you're dealing with. It's right in front of you, in black and white, with loud rock and roll playing and a flashing neon sign moving to the beat of the music yet it is still not seen. The denial on the part of the sufferer matches the denial of those around the alcoholic. The alcoholic truly believes, albeit delusionally, that one day he or she will regain control. That's what insidious is. And the one's closest to the alcoholic simply believe and falsely hope that one day their own alcoholic that they love will regain control.

And the doctors?

If you present all of the symptoms to them and tell them about the drinking their response is typically "Don't drink."

Unless of course the doctor happens to be an alcoholic. Preferably recovered and knowledgeable about this deep rooted sickness. This is why an alcoholic who gets sober and finds a solution to that initial disconnect can be the most effective with other alcoholics who are trying to get sober.

My father, my step mother, and even my step sisters never had a chance when I moved in with them. They didn't know what they were getting into. Neither did I for that matter. We just didn't know. And when it all reached a boiling point, and the fuse I brought with me that was lit when I moved in finally hit my own stick of dynamite, I was offered two words by my step mother.

You guessed it?

"Get out!"

Funny how the story of an alcoholic is predictable. And sad that nearly every person has been touched by such a fiercely misunderstood illness.

Back to Mom's house...

16 - THE INVASION

A parent's love is innate; it's already there when a child is born. I believe that whole "My child can do no wrong" can be labeled as delusional and that it can be shattered in a moment but I don't believe a parent's love for their own child can be shattered or taken away. It's a natural component in the relationship.

When my step mother screamed those two words there was no arguing against my departure from their home. There was no waiting until the morning or a cooling off period where each of us would be allowed to retreat to our own corners for a breather. It wasn't just the two words that were screamed. It was a total "I pushed her over that edge and too far as though if I was allowed another chance and permitted to stay there she would lose her own sanity" thing. This I can see clearly. My father was powerless to fight it. I had to go.

And the same way my father was called by me to "Please come get me" I would place an identical call to my mother just minutes later and ask the same of her.

"Please come get me." Dejected and deflated.

"What is wrong?" Mom's have that way.

"Please come and get me." I repeated with a code that lent the message that I couldn't explain. Shit, I didn't even know what the hell just happened. I was under the impression that everything was perfect. People that think without sound reasoning rarely think anything is wrong with them.

"Okay." Click. She arrived a short time later.

I hadn't seen my mother, sister and Papa during the time I was gone. Life had moved on for the three of them and as my father and step mother didn't know what they were getting into when I went to live with them neither did they. It's been that way most of my life. It's like no one in the family really understood me. I'm not trying to convince anyone to feel bad for me, it is simply a fact. Besides, who really wants to get next to the black sheep? You might catch something right?

When I returned to my mother's home I was a full blown, as delusional as they come, alcoholic. I was under alcohol's spell and it was my master. As each day landed upon the day before it I was getting progressively worse. And not only with the drinking and drugs. My mind was getting sicker and sicker, more and more delusional. The irony is that even in the face of all that happened so far in my short life and all that was happening at this moment in my life I thought I was winning. I was winning at the game of life.

I was welcomed as warmly back to my mother's house as I was to my father's. Another reboot if you will. Today I understand, and believe, that if the same case, or the flavor thereof, keeps repeating itself over and over, maybe with different circumstances, I am missing the lesson that is supposed to be learned. And here was a repeat again of which I would turn a blind eye to. I missed this omen as well. I was great at reading people and situations outside of myself in an effort to *get what I wanted* in life but dismally poor at reading the signs around me, those messages from God, to return to Him.

The most striking of changes I became aware of was the fact that my sister and mother grew closer and closer during my time away. They became great friends, it was like they became sisters. And I felt like an imposition on all of this.

I returned to all of the classmates I hadn't seen in nearly two years as I was quickly transferred back to the high school that I would have been attending had I never left. Classes were chosen for me, I did not have the benefit of choosing my own, those easier and softer ones. I actually didn't give a damn at this point about school. I only cared about alcohol and drugs, and myself. I believe it was still imagined by my family that I would one day break out of that black sheepdom, go to college and be a rocket scientist so I was enrolled in college prep classes.

"Is that Bobby Bach?" As I entered some of the classes and was tossed back into the fish bowl was the whisper I heard in all of the classes. I fell right back in with everyone as though I had left the week before for a brief hiatus.

I did not hang with the college prep students or the jocks or the goth kids. I gravitated toward the students who loved that loud 80's hair band music. And alcohol. And drugs. The music was just the backdrop during this time, it was the use and abuse of alcohol and drugs that woke me every morning with hope. Hope that indeed today I will master these two enigmas and succeed at life. Each day was all about getting high and drunk.

I still had some ties left in the neighborhood at my father's house, especially with the drug dealer I bought my pot from. The dealer that I got a bag from who played Dungeons and Dragons with my father and step mother. Surreal, I know.

Dan would front me ounces at a time and I spent my evenings rolling joints listening to Rush's "Caress of Steel" or "2112." I was preparing to do business the next day at school. I probably would have made enough money to buy a car if I hadn't smoked all of the profit. Then again this is why I was selling joints in school, to feed my habit.

I continued to muscle my way through each day, a godless creature, and tried the best I could to keep that mask squarely planted on my face. But I was failing. Each day brought more and more pain as my resentments morphed into downright visceral anger which led to outright violent temper tantrums. Holes began to appear on the walls of my bedroom and throwing things across the room and holding my mother and sister hostage with these actions, with looks of terror on their faces, became more and more frequent.

I got jobs in restaurants, lost jobs in restaurants, got other jobs in other restaurants and was fired from other jobs in restaurants and for the most part just walked away from jobs if I didn't get my way. I even left jobs if the idea of drinking became overwhelming. Hey, a choice had to be made. An alcoholic has to choose the drink over everything else right? I was a committed alcoholic.

Toward the end of my drinking I worked for a gas station in one of those little cubes, those three by six foot cubes that had space for one person. I couldn't work for, or with, other people anymore. I became a loner of sorts, unless of course we were partying together. My goal in the "cube" was to see how many of my friends I could jam in there. And before we all piled in we made sure a case of beer was planted under the counter.

Thoughts of suicide, and the verbal expression of it, became more and more frequent for me toward the end. The verbal expression used against my family members as threats. I had a friend Paul, I called him "Paulie," who spoke about suicide all the time. He was really depressed and could write some killer poetry. I always tried to get him high to lighten his mood. I gravitated toward him because he seemed to be in a state of mind far darker than mine and seemed to carry the message "There's nothing wrong with you" or "See, you're not that bad." Yeah I had that "I was better than you" attitude down too.

We sat in this cube one day after school smoking pot and comparing our dark lives with one another. He spoke about suicide and I was trying to talk him out of it again. I played a song for him, an uplifting tune from Rush, "Take a Friend," and tried with all that I had in me to lighten his mood. When the song was over he rewound the cassette to the beginning of the song. We painfully waited for the tape to rewind and then he played it again. I sat there all proud of myself thinking I had reached him. When the number ended he had *his* conversation with me.

He explained that I was killing myself with the drinking and the drugs. That until I could get free from it my life would continue to get worse and worse at every level. This was the last time the two of us spoke with one another and I have no idea what became of him.

The thing about this entire interaction brings up two points in the story. One, when another person pointed out the damage my drinking was causing I was done with them. They were dismissed. And two, I missed yet another sign. I missed them all until that fateful weekend I hit bottom.

As my violence in my mother's house grew nastier and nastier there seemed to be a union created between my mother and father. It was born out of two parents trying to find a solution to their common problem, their son. I was brought to a shrink at the local hospital, Bradley Hospital, a division of Butler Hospital, for adolescents. We went there each week, the three of us, and filed into Linda's office to discuss all that was happening with Bobby.

I remember speaking about this with another classmate in school who I grew close to. He started calling me "Fruitcup." I wore that bitch of a nickname like a badge of honor! I think we went to Linda Bell's office on Tuesday nights so when I returned to school on the Wednesday and saw this friend in class he would ask the same question each week.

"How did you make out Fruitcup?"

"Not bad." One week.

"Brutal!" The following week.

It didn't take Linda long to arrive at an

assessment of the situation. Now allow me to precede this with the fact that neither she, nor my mother or my father, knew how much drinking and drugging was going on. There were no piss tests or blood tests and the examinations each week were based on the mind. Alcohol, drugs and most certainly God were never mentioned during these sessions. When the assessment was offered she actually pinned all of my behaviors and attitudes on my parents. She pretty much held them accountable for my behavior. While they may have shared some responsibility for passing on those ideas, emotions, and attitudes, much like I have done with my own children, the shrink failed at uncovering the root of the trouble with me. I got off free and clear, my parents not so much. We never spoke about any of this, even to this day, but I'm led to believe that they must have felt their own sense of bewilderment. The same I was experiencing.

Much like I wore that "Fruitcup" name like a badge I was proud to announce this finding to my friend the very next day. And after he asked what happened I told him it was all my parent's fault. The perfect stance for any alcoholic to take. Blaming others became another layer of my character I would not transcend for years, even after I got sober.

Needless to say that was the last appointment.

As my violence continued to grow I continued to spiral. I now recognize that violence as my physical reaction to not getting my way and being misunderstood. By others and by myself. I remember one evening when I was sitting in the living room with my mother and sister. As I sat there smoking a cigarette reviewing my tax return that someone prepared for me I noticed that an error was made on it.

"What a fucking idiot!" As my thoughts took on spoken words.

"I didn't do anything wrong!!!" My sister screamed from her side of the room thinking I was talking about her.

"I wasn't fucking talking about you!" As we quickly began an argument.

I don't recall what was said after that as the crystal-like blue ashtray that I was using was thrown across the room as hard as I could throw it. It smashed into pieces two feet above my sister's head and showered her with shards of glass. I can't remember the rest of that night.

My thoughts and threats of suicide escalated, intensifying to a fever pitch taking on a daily participation in my life. Where alcohol and drugs were once the medication that seemed to hold me together it no longer worked. It just intensified those lost and lonely feelings I had within me the day I walked into the woods as a naive young kid. I began to withdraw from everyone around me. I just wanted to be alone. I wanted to be drunk. I wanted to be high. I wanted to die and felt dead inside. Inside my mind. And my soul grew darker.

One night I barricaded myself in my bedroom. No one could get in. My mother called my father and when he arrived he practically tore the door off of the room to get in. His first reaction was a closed fist in my face. Something I would have welcomed. A chance to feel physical pain rather than the now torturous mental, emotional and spiritual anguish that would not loosen its grip on me.

I degenerated into a physical shell with no conscience. I was dead inside. And still it wasn't enough pressure to go back to God. Growing up there were a great many things I swore I would never do in my life. As the spiritual malady grew deeper and my mind maddened those became a distant memory and any care, any morals, and values that might have been handed to me as I hit the bumpers in the pinball machine washed away and anything became acceptable in my effort to find release from the pain I felt. I was now looking for another solution and suicide seemed the only option. It would be like this nearly twenty-seven years later when I was twenty-six years sober.

It was the 1980's and Ronald Reagan was in office. His wife Nancy took on the whole "war on drugs" and she was pretty vocal about it. We had commercials on television telling us our brains on drugs could be compared to an egg in a hot frying pan. Parents and teachers and counselors used words like "tough love."

I would lounge around, all blown out, and watch MTV, back when they played music videos, and Nancy Reagan would appear on the screen telling us not to do drugs. In my mind I would battle with this little spitfire. Eventually I would curse her and rest on the word "Bitch" to describe her.

"Just say no." She would say, trying to convince everyone.

"Yeah right!" That's what's holding me together lady.

"Just say no."

"I can't stop Nancy!" And I couldn't stop.

"Just say no."

"Bitch!"

"Just say no." Hitting me at a deeper and deeper level, the commercial now long gone from sight but lingering.

"You don't understand." As I started to understand that I was without the power to stop.

"Just say no."

"You don't fucking get it you little fuck, I can't fucking stop." as I came to understand a part of my problem.

"Just say no." The relentless thought, the seed, planted in my mind.

"I can't stop this madness, I'm fucked." With resignation to the beginning of an understanding that now had no choice but to grow from that seed to a seedling to a bud to a bloom that would be part of that crack in my mask and open wider the fissure that was now growing. A fissure that would lead me to reach out for help.

I fell in love with acid and made this a part of my repertoire. The first time I did it was when I lived with my father. I laughed and laughed and laughed my ass off. Actually it *felt* like my face was laughing off, literally. It felt like my face would crack, not my *mask*. I loved this drug.

I remember coming home, tripping wildly, and going downstairs. My father was sitting alone and watching "The World According To Garp." I sat in the chair, my father and I alone in the living room, a rarity. There was a table between us with a lamp that blocked our view from one another. The lamp was good for two reasons. It filled the inevitable empty space in our conversation and I didn't want him to know I was tripping my balls off.

This is not a movie you watch while tripping especially when you're trying to conceal it. I sat there trying to contain my laughter and was successful for a little while. And then a plane crashed into the house that Robin Williams was thinking about buying. As he and John Lithgow, dressed as a woman, stood there in the yard, a small plane came into view and all of a sudden flew into the house and landed perfectly in one of the rooms on the second floor. The pilot got out of the plane and looked at the two of them standing below on the grass as if what just happened was normal and expected. It was Robin William's next line that shot me into a fit of laughter that further sent me reeling into a deeper fit of uncontrollable laughter.

"What are the odds it'll be hit again?" I obscured this metaphor with my tripping laughter.

I got up and excused myself and said good night to my father. He always knew when I was stoned, I just couldn't hide it nor did I care to. I think he probably knew this wasn't his usual stoned son, and that something else was at play here.

There was the night my friend Kevin and I were going to a party and wanted to do something trippy. We made our way over three towns into the projects that were a "drive-thru" for whatever you needed. They called it Crook Manor. You pulled through and the dealers would hang out of the windows yelling for your "order."

Our plan was to cop something and head to a party. It usually took an hour or so to start tripping and a few more to hit that "peak." So we went to the Manor earlier in the afternoon. Neither one of us had ever been there so we were blindly looking for this place. After driving around for a half hour with no success Kevin was ready to give up. Me, not so much. Alcoholics, drug addicts, that's how we are. Once that plan is set we like to stick to it. The problem I felt we were having was the fact that you really can't walk into a gas station or convenience store and ask for directions to the neighborhood that sells drugs.

As Kevin finally gave up and he set to starting our way back to the ramp to get back on the highway I saw a man walking down the street. Desperation was settling in nicely and I would have done anything to get what my mind was already set upon. And I did. With a sense of panic I told Kevin to slow down.

"Hey you!" I yelled out of the window with a desperation that matched the desperate look of the man walking down the street.

He answered: "What?"

"Can you tell us where Crook Manor is?" Like I was a tourist looking for the hottest dinner spot and hadn't had a meal in a month.

"Yeah, it's......

"Get in!"

I couldn't get the car door opened quick enough.

He jumped in, showed us to our destination, and we were off. I think we just left him there in the projects. We drank all night and made it to two parties. As we drove home to my mother's house we were pulled over by the police. It was one of those guys with the white shirts. Not the typical blue ones.

This one had some rank. Kevin was smashed and whispered "Oh shit." I went from that happy place to dog-shitting-razor-blades fearful as soon as the lights came on behind us. The booze was all gone so no problem there. That's why we were headed home, no more booze.

Kevin was asked to walk a straight line behind the vehicle while I didn't dare to move a hair on my body while frozen in the passenger's seat. I heard Kevin laugh at the officer and tell him "I can't. I'm too drunk." Hey, he was honest with the officer. He was told to stay behind the car and then the officer appeared next to me on the bench seat asking if we had drugs in the car. I was not as honest as Kevin and said "No" while sitting on a bag of weed. He ripped our cigarette packs apart, looked around and then got out of the car. He returned to Kevin and asked him where we going. Kevin told him we were headed to my house just a short distance away. He let us go!

It was a different time back then and looking back I don't think the officer cared for what Nancy Reagan was trying to tell everyone either. We made it back to my mother's house around 2am and laughed all the way home. You might think it ends there, eh?

We pulled into the driveway and there was no way we could walk into the house tripping and drunk like this. My mother had already embraced that whole "tough love" thing they did back then. She was wising up to the *symptoms* in me, the use and abuse of alcohol and drugs. We decided it would be wise to just sleep in the car. So on a hot summer night I took the front seat and he the back.

After some time we finally crashed.

The next morning with the hot sun slamming the

car and dutifully baking us inside more so than we were baked the night before my mother woke us up. She wasn't pleasant, knocking on the windows and inviting us in for a home-cooked breakfast. She had the garden hose and proceeded to fill the car with water. I'm not sure what we did that day but let me assure you that I most definitely would have been looking to repeat the night before.

Kevin was one of the two I walked into the woods with to smoke my first joint. I haven't seen him since I got clean and sober.

A friend of mine, who recently passed away, and I became fast friends while in high school. We were inseparable. We both loved music and loved to party together. We created what we called "Blueberry Fields." This would become a Friday night party in the woods with a campfire open to anyone who wanted to come by.

We took orders for booze all week in school and had a friend of ours do our shopping when we got out of school. We iced the booze down in the woods and sold sixes of beer to anyone who needed it.

I remember walking through the halls of the school and everyone would be screaming "Blueberry Fields." I knew I had arrived when those two words became affixed to my ego and persona.

He and I did acid every Monday in school. They actually called all of this garbage we would gladly eat without thought mescaline back then. I delusionally deduced that "M" was for mescaline and "M" was for Monday therefore Monday *must* be mescaline day. We would call each other early in the morning to confirm that we each took our hit.

We didn't share any classes together but one. He enjoyed his trip alone most of the day as did I. We just happened to be in gym class together and it met just before lunch when we were peaking. Our classmates never knew what violent ping pong was until we arrived to class and demonstrated this for them. He was one of the few friends I would stay in touch with after leaving school and he visited me every Sunday when I was in rehab.

Those were some of the fun trips. Not all were that enjoyable. I ate this stuff and would make the mistake of revealing it to someone who was tired of my crap already. This just ripped the whole thing apart and usually led to me eating more of it. I nearly beat the shit out of my best friend while on a tab of thc. (I don't even know if it was thc.) The point is I didn't care to know what I was eating. I was looking for the straightest distance between reality and oblivion and some of these drugs kept me in the fast lane while riding in that car.

The one line in the song "Empty Spaces" by Pink Floyd that still resonates with me to this day is "Mother, why'd it have to be so high?" It was this movie that led to my decision to reach out for help to get clean and sober. We're getting to that.

At the time that Nancy was insisting we all "Just Say No" there was some covert work being done within the high school to get to the bottom of the drinking and drugs. Our vice principal was a pretty effective leader. In the end he became a great confidant for me.

Many of my friends were selling dope in the

school. Joints and small bags. Joints for a buck, bags for five or ten bucks. What we didn't know is that there were officers on the campus posing as students and they were watching all of us. They had cameras set up all over the place as well. By the time we all caught the wind of this news, it was too late. We were caught and cornered before they actually dropped the hammer.

The day each of us were singled out in our classrooms the word passed through the halls quickly as to who just got pinched. As I sat in that same class with the classmate that gave me the name "Fruitcake," during a study hall period where you do nothing if you have no elective or activity, they came in. I used these dead periods to sleep off a high and was drooped over my tall drafting table.

The two officers, those "students," came in with the vice principal and removed me from the class.

Before we go there let me share what happened the week before. Everyone in the school was called back to their homerooms at the end of the day for some reason. I sat there at my desk waiting impatiently to get out of school.

"C'mon, ten more fucking minutes!" I was thinking.

The back door of the class opened and the vice principal called me out of the room. We went into the next classroom, conveniently empty, and I was told that they, he and a teacher, wanted to search me. I must have looked like a deer caught in headlights. I had a bag of dope and a pack of papers on me. And I didn't know my rights.

I agreed and figured this was the end. (It was getting close.) They patted me down and made a comment that there was an awful lot of padding in the shoulders of my jean jacket. Don't judge, it was the eighties and we ate that shit up. They commented like I was Pablo Escobar and I had a kilo of dope sewn into my jacket. This pissed me off.

As they continued their pat down they felt the front pockets of my jeans. The goods were in my front left pocket. When they asked "What is that?" I knew I was toast and mentally surrendered. I reached into my pocket and was about to say it was a "*small* bag and papers" when I felt the tip of my lighter. I grabbed the lighter, pulled it out and handed it to them. I walked away from that one free.

Now when these two other fellows pulled me into a teacher's lounge and told me they wanted to search me I agreed without hesitation. Besides we were all wise to what was happening now. We were all laying low but were still waiting to see what would happen with those so-called cameras. As they started to give me instructions and tell me what they wanted me to do I began to move without hesitation.

As I looked defiantly at the vice principal never breaking eye contact with him I kicked my boots off. I ripped my socks off. I tore my shirt off and dropped my pants. My reaction to the search by the officers was far different than to his search and he knew immediately what he had missed the last time. He also knew that I knew it was coming. I had three 20$ bills on me and they asked why. I just got paid from work so there you have it.

I was escorted out of one building and into the next to have my locker searched. When they opened my locker there was nothing in there. As we moved about the school to yet another locker I shared with another classmate I overheard them speaking about the other students that would be given the same honor and treatment and then the question was asked whether I would be able to tip them off.

And then the fruit of their cameras came into view. And it wasn't good.

When the word came to us how the videos from the cameras would be handled they didn't call us into an office at the school. They didn't tell us one by one. They strategically sent letters to our parents at home. They arrived on a Friday.

When I arrived home my sister presented me with the news with a smile on her face that said "You're fucked." It was *not* that smile she flashed at my father's apartment years before when I asked my father that granddaddy of a question. This one was filled with malice, and hate. Contempt. I was told to stay home by my mother as she and my sister had to go do my sister's paper route. You might guess what I did next. I ran. And besides I had this party I was going to and a list of product that people were counting on me to bring. I didn't get home until the next night. I had zero respect for my mother or her home, as fractured and chaotic and sick as it was. I was a part of that sickness and I certainly added to it.

The police invited all of us and our parents to the station for the show. We all had to be there at the same time. My mother refused to go and it fell on my father to escort me there. We arrived and sat in one of the benches in the courtroom. All of my friends were there and our usual high-fiving-what's-up-with-you greetings were squelched. That definitely wasn't happening.

They started the tapes and one by one we all

appeared on the film. As each of us made our appearance we would sink in our bench wanting to crawl on the floor. Not only did they show us the video they described each of our actions in them. I was filmed selling a bag of dope to this car that pulled up at the school. I knew something was wrong while I was making the sale and something inside told me not to do it but it's easy to prey on teenagers naivety.

The result was this...nothing. At least immediately. My father was perturbed that his name was dragged into the police station and that was all. My mother was pretty pissed and her reaction would be one I never saw coming. As committed to that war on drugs as Nancy Reagan was my mother committed to her own war. I have come to name her campaign "Tough Love." And I began to see a side of her that I'd never seen before. As much as I craved yet didn't want anything to do with my parents she was about to be everything in a mother I craved. And that was love. Love for another human being. Love for a family member. Love for a son.

And I wouldn't like it. Though as I look back on it now, I loved it.

I was about to see every sign placed before me by God. But let's keep going before we get to my mother's efforts to see her son recover.

I was the guinea pig in my group of friends. As I fell deeper and deeper into the use and abuse of drugs, always looking for the next best high, or escape, medicine cabinets in anyone's house I entered became fair game to me. As I fell deeper and deeper the people in my life would change as well. If they couldn't keep up with me they were casually brushed aside in favor of someone else who could. There was a period, before I moved into my father's home, when I tried anything that was placed before me. I was already on a course of self destruction in an effort to reconstruct myself.

If my friends and I came upon a prescription in your medicine cabinet there was no contemplation as to who would try it first. I would. And if it had an effect that was in line with our goal, oblivion, then I shared it. That sharing didn't last long as my need for oblivion grew within my mind and emotions.

I shared that I didn't know that Nana was sick and in pain as she set about her own effort to ensure our comfort before she died. A short time after she was gone I found a bottle of her 500mg percodan. This was not a small bottle, this baby was packed full and the pills were surprisingly big. I took the bottle. This was probably one of the only times I showed them to my friends. I think there was a fear wrapped around that bottle, as if they might take me out. How's that for irony?

I was thirteen and I had a paper route not far from my mother's house and this was started with the obligatory folding of the papers followed by a one hour stop at another friend's house for some smoking of the joints. Mix in a bit of The Doors or some Deep Purple and it was always a great reprieve from the day.

I shared this paper route with a friend who liked to do drugs and drink the same way I did and we would ride our bicycles along the route tossing the papers on the doorsteps while riding with no hands. If there was any such thing as being a professional paper boy I had that one down pretty good.

Before we made the stop at our friend's for some smoke previous to doing the route we ate some of the percs. I don't recall how many she ate but I know I ate six. 3000mgs of I-have-no-idea-what-I-just-ate-I-just-hope-it-has-a-cool-effect. As we sat and listened to Jim Morrison's poetic pain, love and triumph, my friends pointed out that my face was getting white and my lips purple. My hair was short at this time, those 80's punk-style haircuts being the rage, and my friends told me that the hair on the top of my head was standing straight up.

I dismissed their observations. I refused to believe them. I did feel something from the pills but my mind was wrapped up in looking for the high, not the downside, the side effects you hear about when an ad is on the television for a medication. And besides I thought maybe they were too stoned and were busting my balls. I never got up to look in the mirror. I kept waiting. And waiting and waiting. I couldn't deny the next part as it was all too real for me. It was physically violent.

We left our friends house and proceeded to sling newspapers. As we made our way down the major road, she on her side without the side streets and me on my side with the side streets, I began to puke. This wasn't one of those one and done that I sometimes experienced when drinking only to go immediately back to the drink for some more of that hair of the dog. This was a gut-wrenching nausea I never experienced before. My side of the route had eight side streets. I colored each one of these streets with vomit as I went up and down them. Not just the first two. I left my mark on all of them.

In my mind it wasn't the pills that did this to me.

It was something else. Maybe I took one too many. Maybe the beer I had at my friend's house was it? As these voices set in and my thoughts went to "maybe that fear will be realized and I'll die." My body certainly felt free of pain and lighter than it had in my life. Maybe I would just float away.

I ended the paper route not by going home and crashing out or seeking help. I just kept going throughout the night with the pot to calm me down. I survived and this emboldened me at a deeper level. I never surrendered that need to be the guinea pig.

Over time I developed the constitution of a battleship when it came to alcohol and drugs while I sought some kind of refuge from you and even myself. When it came to being able to make decisions as to when, where, and who I would drink or drug with there was no compass to follow. Only the dictates of that spiritual sickness, that body allergy and mental obsession. When it came to the what and how there really wasn't much of a choice there either. I was at the mercy of something bigger than me now, alcohol and drugs. It's no wonder that the first words I would relate to in an AA meeting were "drunk, junkie and dope fiend." This is what I became in a few short years and I was damn good at it.

Where alcohol and drugs once allowed me relief from my mind and the ability to shut reality out as if it were controllable with an on/off switch I lost this benefit. All of those objectionable things I wished to escape from came back and were before me front and center. My mind became a steel trap and many things were wrestling within this device for attention. Ugliness writhing around for my attention. The fears.

The resentments. And even the harms that I was doing to others through my own self-propelled effort to be the evader of reality and an exception to the rule, and rules. Those rules of nature. I was hitting bottom and when I met it there would be pain as I had the alcohol and drugs removed from me.

ROBERT ERNEST BACH

17 - THE TRIAL

The title of this chapter is from the Pink Floyd film "The Wall." The part that includes an interaction between a mother and a son. And it would be this pivotal interaction between my mother and I that would begin to tip the scales for me to favor some help and surrender to the fact that I was powerless over alcohol and drugs.

As I spiraled out of control and the alcohol and drugs failed to come close to serving as a method of release from the pain within, my mother gained a strength I wouldn't fully appreciate until writing this out. She stepped up to the plate as a mother and hit one straight out of the park.

The best gift I ever received while drinking was a jug of Southern Comfort. It came from my neighbor who, in his own turn, would seek treatment for alcohol and drug abuse. He would be the one to place that call to me to take me to one of those "meetings." The night I called another friend and insisted he get his ass to the house so we could get high before we went.

I had grown so belligerent and uncaring at the end of my drinking. I don't believe I could have deepened those shortcomings. The gallon of SoCo became known to me as "The Last Resort." I think my friend thought I would kill the bottle in a night but I didn't. I proudly displayed it on my dresser in my bedroom. I was seventeen when I received this gift and had not one care in me that I was showing no respect to my mother or home, fully, at this point. I put it there like a dare. "I *dare* you to tell me to get rid of it" was my attitude.

Like the Christmas that I held my mother's holiday hostage. A Christmas celebrated in the same home that we celebrated the first Christmas without my father. It was like I was determined to change the flavor and depth of the holiday to suit my own perverted and twisted thinking. As if I could alter the past and maybe even my view of it *while drinking.*

My mother had Christmas planned out so that she, my sister, and I could spend Christmas Eve together before we had Papa over the next day for dinner. If you're a parent of teenagers you might know what it's like to try and get your children to stay home when all they want to do is be away from you. If you don't have teenagers maybe you once were like this at that age. As she expressed that she wanted us home my mind went to work.

"I could use this to my advantage, my agenda." Is what I felt.

I told her I would stay home *if* she got me a bottle of Kahlua. I was such an asshole and must have been so convincing that she did this for me.

Then again at some level those closest to the alcoholic fall victim to its madness as well. As much as the alcoholic dreams of regaining control over their own consumption so do those around the alcoholic. They erroneously believe that they can control the amount and circumstances surrounding the alcohol and the alcoholic. In many respects the spouses, parents, and family members of the alcoholic become just as sick as the drinker. I share this out of experience, my own and the many men and women, and their families, I have met and worked with.

I sat in the chair, the one that saw the shower of glass shards from the ashtray thrown over my sister's head with a feeling of victory as I drank my Kahlua on the rocks. Thank God she bought the larger bottle was all I could think. Notice I thanked *God* for this miracle. Maybe He was on my side after all. My mother sat in the same room also feeling the victor as she had her son home through an agreeable compromise. This is where our relationship had come in a short time.

The Southern Comfort you ask? Why "The Last Resort?"

From nearly the beginning of my drinking I had the fear of doing without alcohol. It terrified me. I remember a weekend my friend and I spent with my uncle and his partner out on the shore in Clinton, Connecticut. This happened when I lived with my father.

We packed our bags, and a lot of dried goods. The pot. We spent the weekend sunning and eating and being thrilled for some freedom from the neighborhood. What we didn't imagine was going through all of our dope before the weekend ended.

That is a horrible place for an alcoholic to be. To be without a substance that is wholly depended on. It's a horror show in the mind more explosive in theatrics and darkness than "The Rocky Horror Picture Show." This is where that idea of not compromising ones morals and values comes into play for the alcoholic. Hence lying, cheating and stealing become acceptable. It's expected from alcoholics, doing those things they, myself included, swore would never be done. The sad fact is that it can still hold true even after the alcohol is removed in some. It was this way for me for many years even while clean and sober.

Once we were out of pot and I sat around waiting for my uncle to offer his up and maybe get us high I grew restless and forlorn. Naturally I started to look around the place and quickly found the bar and made a drink. Why stop there? I found a vial of coke while searching a bedroom upstairs and banged that out pretty quickly. I didn't share the coke with my friend. The days of sharing were over by the time I was fifteen.

The bottle of Southern Comfort was there as a buffer to those hard times that I failed to realize capturing booze or drugs to keep going. If I failed to find someone to feed my addiction I always had this bottle to fall back on. It was empty and long gone by the time I left for treatment.

Toward the end of my drinking and as my mother escalated her campaign of "Tough Love" she would reach into her arsenal for any weapon she thought might bring a destruction to my madness.

I would be laying in my room listening to music with depressing lyrics as my now comfortable and familiar swamp of self-pity was interrupted. She would come to my room and tell me there was a guy outside who wanted to speak with me. One day it was a gentleman who worked for an employee assistance program who would tell me the downfall that comes with alcohol and drug use. I sat and listened with a dismissive smirk on my face with thoughts like "No shit man, you're preaching to the choir."

The next would be a state trooper dressed from head to toe in his sharp, and somewhat intimidating, uniform speaking to what would happen if laws were exacted with regard to my activities. This had zero effect as you really can't scare or strike fear into an alcoholic. It just doesn't work or if it does its temporary. And besides the only fear that struck my core was doing without, without drugs or alcohol.

I was quickly sentenced to a counselor who spoke to what actually happens when alcohol or specific drugs enter the body. It was informational only for me. Almost like an after the fact education that explained some of the crazy physical and mental reactions I had while drinking or doing drugs. My attitude was "Thank you very much."

I grew into that part of the sickness that requires me to just be alone. I had no desire to be with anyone, unless of course it involved some form of seeking oblivion. I landed in that pit of despair and my thoughts ran to wanting to check out many times throughout the day. I would dream of not being alive and feeling the freedom of not being here anymore. Never did a thought go to how this would affect others around me and if they did it was easily replaced with the idea that they'd be better off without me. It would be twenty-six years before I would land at this same place. It would be about twenty-seven years later that I would watch "It's a Wonderful Life" alone one evening after that huge spiritual upheaval and would be reduced to uncontrollable sobs and a puddle of tears.

I tried as hard as I could to hide from that tornado within but couldn't escape reality at this point. It was a futile effort, and tiring. I was toast and I was done.

I managed to make it to my senior prom on a Friday night and didn't even go to it with my girlfriend whom I would eventually marry. A few of us, the few of us who cared only to explore that place of oblivion, couldn't wait to ditch our dates and get out of there and party it up. That pre-graduating high school celebration of "we made it, we are free." I wouldn't even make it another week.

I don't remember too much of this weekend. I do know I didn't see my mother, sister or family for the next three days. Most of it was spent in a blackout.

The night of the prom I recall waking up from the blackout three times and each time I was roused from this absurd trance I was with different people. It *was* like time travelling. I don't recall leaving the venue or parting ways with my date. The next thing I knew I was at my friend Michele's house. As we left the house I saw this table that might be of use to us throughout the night. I picked up the glass top table with the chrome spiral base and casually carried it away. The glass would be useful for doing lines. She, her father, and I would laugh as this memory was brought up one day not too long ago before he passed away.

The next time I woke up was as the sun was rising and I was in my friend's Firebird. I clearly remember that the sky was the same exact color as his car; the coolest shade of blue. And then back to sleep.

The next time I woke up was while traveling down route 2 in RI in the backseat of a yellow Saab. And then back to sleep.

It was now Saturday.

I don't recall the rest of that day. Later in the evening we were at another friend's house whose parents were away for the weekend or a couple of weeks. Where they were or for how long was of no importance to me. What was important was that the party continue on. I don't remember much of that night except some time spent with the girlfriend.

And then Sunday.

I woke up the next day late in the afternoon to some pretty weird looks and a killer hangover. A hangover that seemed to permeate my emotions and mind and into my core. Most likely the looks were of disgust. It was suggested that I go home to which I replied "I don't have a home anymore." I didn't leave their house. Alcoholics are like that too. I could move into any place in a heartbeat and make it my own. I can only suppose we partied some more later that day and into the night because I can't remember.

It was now Monday. The day I picked up the telephone and placed a call to my mother pleading for help.

I woke up in my friend's house that morning as they were getting ready for school and quickly passed right out. I wasn't going to school. When I eventually came to I called the school and asked to speak with my confidant, the vice principal. When he answered I told him I couldn't get to school.

"Why can't you come to school?" He asked patiently. The man was a saint went it came to that virtue.

"I'm having a problem with my family." Was all I could think to spit out to him and then hung up. I was still using the excuse of "it's my family's fault."

I would go into a treatment facility the following morning after finally bottoming out later that day.

After school whatever friends I had left at this point came by my friend's house and decided to watch Pink Floyd's "The Wall." I had seen this trippy, tragic and surreal drama many times before this day. Sometimes drunk, sometimes stoned, sometimes tripping on acid and sometimes under the influence of all three at the same time. On this day I was just a little stoned from some pot. I couldn't drink anymore, I was just too physically sick.

There was a fissure in my being that couldn't be closed and my mask was laid on the floor. I was open for the first time in years, and I started to see and hear things differently. I noticed there was a spirit of compassion in the room being extended toward me. It wasn't that typical "look at me" and "I need to be the center of attention and the universe" way about me that noticed this. It was something different. I didn't know this then but as I look back I can see it. I think my friends knew the jig was up for me. And on some deep parallel I knew it as well.

We watched the movie and my friends laughed and talked. I don't know what they were laughing about. I don't know what they were speaking to as I was now seeing this movie in a way I never did before. I was being *shifted*.

I could identify and relate to the main character. His break from what he was born with. His choices. His experience. His eventual degradation of emotion and the annihilation of his mental faculties. His impending bottom. His submission to something that had him in its grip. His ability to push everyone away. His sense of aloneness in a crowded room. His lack of care. His personality change brought about by circumstances and his use and abuse of alcohol. His short-lived and delusional triumphal feeling that he was winning at the game of life. His eventual rescue.

And then the moment when a lyric is sung that expresses that a change in uniform has to happen. This one hit me and I knew deep in my core that I had failed dismally at playing God. That the God-shirt was indeed too big for me to fill. I needed to let go of that part of His uniform I had been trying to wear.

And like the character Pink I would need to go away to be freed. Freed from the alcohol and the drugs and the madness of my mind.

The last part of the movie that describes the exposure of someone before their peers in order to be broken down and released from the bondage of self, the ego, wouldn't be realized in me for a while. It would be my return to the movie months later when the last part called "The Trial" matched the description of my experience in the treatment center.

I missed the last part of the flick that day as I was reduced to a puddle of tears. It was at this moment that I now know God, casually sitting before that giant game set He holds sway over, allowed me to see and feel His Grace. He focused His attention on me as I now turned my attention to Him. The game of hide and seek where I always sought to hide from Him and He always sought to capture my attention with those signs, those omens, was now over. I was to begin my journey back home to Him in ways that are as unimaginable as faith in Him is mysterious.

I picked up the phone and reached out to my mother after a long weekend away from home. I was still crying and she asked what was wrong with the same concern she offered a couple of years before when I called and asked her to pick me up at my father's house.

I had to *ask for help*. A very foreign concept to me. I understand now that asking for help is an extension of willingness. As I explained that I needed help, as though she might need to know this and might not be aware of what has been happening with me for six years, she listened. She explained that there were "two beds available" for me. One on the grounds of that IMH or a treatment facility. I asked to go to the latter as a my friend who gave me "The Last Resort" had gone there. I wanted something that might have an air of familiarity to it.

She explained that I had to go now and I pleaded with her to just let me stay home one night before I went. And that I had two things that needed to be done before leaving. She agreed to this and I'm confident that with what I know now she must have made some pleading phone calls for me to keep that bed open.

I hung up the phone and looked to my friend.

"What do you want to do, what can I do for you?" was the question asked by the expression on his face.

"Can you give me a ride?" I asked.

"Let's go!" As he sprang into action.

I asked him to bring me to my girlfriend's house. I thought she deserved at least an explanation of what was about to happen as I left for thirty days. We arrived at her house and after speaking with her I asked if I could use a phone to call my father. I called my father and explained what had happened and that I needed to go away. I don't recall what he said yet do remember his patience as he listened to his son.

My friend took me home after this and as we drove I asked him for some pot so that I could get through the night and the following morning. He handed me a package and dropped me off at home.

I went into the house and there weren't any words spoken by anyone that I can recall. I went into my bedroom and laid down for a while and thought about what I was going to do. I felt relief and never did a doubt come before me pleading with me to abandon this plan.

Later in the night I showered and smoked a joint in the bathroom with a towel placed at the base of the door so that my mother and sister wouldn't smell it. Never did I get so high from pot before this and I welcomed the escape for a while.

At some point Papa must've been told of the plan as he arrived the next morning to take the ride to the southern part of the state with my mother, sister and me. Before we left there was one other place I needed to visit. My friend returned in the morning and escorted me to the high school. I went in the vice principal's office and told him what I was doing and that I had to leave the school. He wished me well and

I left.

I was driven to treatment on the early morning of June 3rd, 1986 just shy of three months after my eighteenth birthday. Two weeks before I was due to graduate high school. I didn't know a thing about alcoholism, addiction or spiritual illness/malady. Somewhere in my delusional mind I actually believed that I was going to drinking school. I thought that while I was away I would be given the means to learn how to win this game of life and that they would be teaching me how to drink safely and how to control it. I just didn't know. And I didn't know that I didn't know. It was a compounded ignorance like the compounded delusions I had (nearly my entire life).

My mother was under the impression that my problem was isolated to drugs and didn't know the extent of my drinking. As this was a facility that treated alcoholism she told me to lie about how much I drank. She asked me to embellish the truth. I didn't need to embellish a thing.

When I walked through the front doors of this facility I was still stoned from the morning, as my friend and I blew a joint when he took me to the school to say good bye.

My mother, sister and Papa drove away. I felt fear as I watched the back of the old Ford Comet go yet also let out a sigh of relief.

I woke up the next morning in a med unit, clean and sober. The first thing I noticed was that the sun was shining.

18 - INTERMEZZO NUMBER FIVE

I came to the twelve steps of Alcoholics Anonymous, steps that have been easily adapted to address many situations that arise out of spiritual sickness, spiritual deficiency. These principles have become the *foundation* of a life that I *must* live spiritually, especially after my spiritual upheaval four years ago. They are magical to me. They formed a path by which I was able to break free. Break free from not only the alcohol and drugs, what became my ultimate symptom born out of my maladjustment with God, but the lower self. They were the basis of putting together a rudimentary formation within to not only begin righting my listless ship of a soul and mind but also to begin the exploration of a new God-consciousness. Awareness.

There is a quote I wish to share with you before we move on further. I realize some may want to call bullshit with those last few chapters. Maybe you are an alcoholic or on the edge of losing control, the power of choice. Or perhaps you live with an alcoholic and the writing was a hit between the eyes and something inside of you wishes to wrap itself around denial. I get it. As an alcoholic I am more than familiar with denial. I lived it well before I picked up a drink, while drinking and for many years clean and sober. There are moments, even today, as a recovered alcoholic that I can easily drift into denial when I lose my mind's eye and fall back into a trance. That lack of awareness. The disconnect from God. The loss of God-consciousness.

The quote?

"There is a principle which is a bar against all information, which is proof against all arguments and which cannot fail to keep a man in everlasting ignorance - that principle is contempt prior to investigation."[2]

It's attributed to the author William Paley, a British philosopher.

The part I wish to call your attention to is the actual principle, "contempt prior to investigation." The line he actually wrote was "Contempt prior to examination is an intellectual vice, from which the greatest faculties of mind are not free."[3]

This describes how I've spent most of my life. Playing God. I was always quick to enter a judgment or criticism, witty comment or sarcastic reaction before fully investigating what it was I was judging. Whether it was you, an object, an institution, a principle, a race, an ethnic background, fill in the blank, and the list goes on and on and on. Can you relate to this?

I've come to understand this part of my character

---

[2] See Bibliography

[3] See Bibliography

that wishes to pull that God-shirt on at so many intricate levels each with their own nuances. And it's not always been a pleasant experience, these discoveries about my own flaws and character. As a matter of fact there were multiple awakenings as I typed this manuscript. Some were pleasing and some were real eye-openers.

What I've come to understand is that playing God is not just limited to alcoholics, we all do it as humans, spirits walking around in our meatsuits. My wish to play God in life, whether by trying to control others, through those judgments and criticisms, sarcasm or condemnation will always keep me bound to my lower self, my ego. I'll never be free as long as these attitudes are permitted.

The twelve steps require a full self-examination by each who would journey through them yet there is resistance to do this work. Understandably so, it's not easy. It further requires that this be shared about. Not in an open forum but with another spirit wrapped in a meatsuit, and God.

It was through just these two principles that I was able to see my own deficiencies. I was able to find that my cemented ideas, emotions, and attitudes were of no use to me and I was given but a glimpse of the guiding forces that were set up in me. The writing I've done so far and the sharing I've done with you has lent more understanding on how those guiding forces were carried out and I'm rightly imagining that this will continue for me until I feel no gas left in the tank at my keyboard.

I still have many years of experience to share with you about my spiritual journey and I would ask that you reserve your judgment until we are finished together. I'm asking you to suspend your own contempt until you fully investigate what is written in its entirety between the front and back cover of this book.

I've learned that once my reconnection to God was established it came with His discipline. For many years I was but an empty vessel. This includes the period of time before I began drinking, while I was drinking and even a great amount of the time I was clean and sober after I left the treatment facility. I had no conscience when it came to many things. It was impossible to feel any guilt, shame or remorse.

I spoke to those predictions that the founders wrote about that come with the necessary work of their steps. I spoke to this in one of our "Intermezzos." It was their experience where they found that no matter what had happened and no matter how low they fell in their own lives in the realm of morals and values they discovered that those experiences ultimately benefitted another person. It was put to great use by God. Today I understand that He makes the best use out of the worst, never expected, situations at times. I've experienced this exactly.

Another of those predictions based on their experiences spoke to not regretting the past nor wishing to shut it out by closing doors behind us. Admittedly, it is hard to share all of these things about myself and my journey and something tells me it's going to get even heavier. I do not regret my past when it comes to sharing it with other men and women when I work as a tour guide for them, one of God's agents, as they trudge the journey through these principles. This is not to say that I don't feel a deep sense from within when a memory falls into my mind that brings with it a guilt that might be overwhelming, a shame that wishes to drive me to hide for a while, or a remorse for something that can never be righted, amended. I get these three on occasion, sometimes one will show, other times two will appear walking hand in hand, and still other times two will invite the third to pay a visit.

I've come to know, come to believe, that this is God's Grace. The visitation of a memory wrapped in a feeling on the bottom of the scale. No, I don't think His Grace is always soft, mushy and sugarcoated. Most times His Grace is recognized as a lesson by me. And that ultimate lesson is to trust and rely on Him without fail, absolutely. That is indeed a tall order. The irony is that as I have been writing there have been repeated instances of these rogue feelings that accompanied my thoughts and ruminations.

I could have written chapter after chapter after chapter about my drinking and drug use yet believe I have made my qualification as an alcoholic clear. I wish to do the same with regard to the solution I found in the coming chapters.

I may visit this idea of "contempt prior to investigation" before we finish this journey together but let me share one other point on it.

Remember I spoke to the value I placed on my kneecaps when a group of men told me I would go through the steps or they would shoot them off? I spoke to getting into them without hesitation. And I did. And there was no doubt that there was Something there yet I didn't follow the directions that are laid out in that initial piece of literature the pioneers published. I was brought through with a different method. Like a "let's just scratch the surface" application. An application that would fail to produce a bang-zoom personality change in me and leave me floundering for many, many years in recovery doomed to repeat my past over and over and over. The most detrimental of which would include passing on to my own children the ideas, emotions, and attitudes that were passed on to me. I would continue to cause pain for others, for years, sober.

When another man answered the call and acted as a tour guide to take me through these principles as the pioneers had laid them out in 1939 I would enjoy a perfect release. And a perfect reconnect to God. And it all happened rather quickly. Four months tops.

It would be months after this as I tried to live by these principles, this "design for living," that I would experience a downfall and slip into my own pit of despair. It was all of the amends that had to be addressed, the amends in the area of financial restitution I would have to walk through. They just seemed insurmountable. Damn near impossible, like there just wasn't enough time to achieve this end.

I grew weary and wanted to check out, again. I felt like my connection with God had been broken as it indeed was. Like God wasn't there anymore. In actuality that ugly selfishness and self-centeredness were back to pay their twisted respect to me. It drove me back to the thoughts of suicide.

A friend of mine recommended that I go speak with someone and at the same time I came upon a meditation that a few of us recovered alcoholics practice. When I paid this therapist a few visits he shared a few things with me as I shared what was going on with me with him.

He shared that I had lived my life with thoughts going directly to my heart and that most of my decisions and reactions to life were quick and without contemplation at all. He shared that this is the tragedy with many humans, not just alcoholics. A thought will come to us and shoot directly to the heart rather than making a pit stop along the way for review. A review to determine which course to take.

He observed that as much as I had done the work and felt an immediate response I was not doing enough "investigation." I wasn't exploring that mystery of faith that would lead to a solid trust and reliance on God forgoing the need to play God.

I wasn't trusting in His plan because it wasn't a tangible thing. I couldn't touch it or read it. I had to learn how to do this as readily as I trusted in the electricity that powers a light bulb. I would have to take some action much like flipping a switch to power that light bulb. I would have to extend that decision to trusting and relying on God with the necessary action. This would involve the process of becoming an agent for Him and His works. But how? That's always the question, eh?

ROBERT ERNEST BACH

PART FOUR

THE END OF MY SECOND LIFE

19 - A NEW BEGINNING

As we begin Part Four of the writing allow me to lend you a glimpse of what will come between us in the way of experience, strength, and hope. Not only would I remain clean and sober I would find God and most times in the most unexpected and unusual places. Sometimes through the coercion of others and most times through the coercion of those twelve steps. All by His Grace.

I will share parts of my life with you as they pertain to becoming God-conscious. And even though I believe God makes use of every bit and piece of our time in our meatsuits the last thing I wish to do is bore you with a lot of fluff. There are many things I will not recall while I was in the rehab for thirty days as some of it was spent in a fog. I'll share what comes to me.

I woke up on June 4th of '86; I didn't *come to* as I had been for a few years. I walked out of my room, within a comfortable hospitable setting on the "med unit," and walked into a common room that had a television. The last thing I watched was "The Wall" and it was still resonating with me. I asked the nurse for some aspirin and a cup of coffee. I was offered breakfast, something that would bring me feelings of nausea when thought about in the past in the morning. Breakfast at one, two or three in the morning became palatable when I was drinking.

As a patient in this facility, High Point in North Kingstown, RI, I would be exposed to a great many men and women who would give of themselves tirelessly to reach a young and naive eighteen year old boy who was by all accounts a shipwreck. A shipwreck as they once were, by abusing alcohol. This facility still stands to this day yet is run under a different name and ownership and at times I've returned to do exactly what was done for me. Pass along the message, with my words and presence, that a full recovery from the illness is indeed attainable if one is willing to do some heavy lifting.

I was shot down one of the winding halls that connected the buildings in the complex within two days and brought to one of the two units. I was assigned to the "East Unit." I would be a resident there until my release on July 5th. I was set to be released on the 4th of July but in my last week there I grew fearful to be released into society on that particular date. I was afraid I would celebrate my freedom with a drink. I've remained clean and sober since, even against every odd.

I was assigned a room and shared this with a man

better than twice my age. We became fast friends and two others were there as well in this close knit circle, uh square. His name was John and the other two were Tom and Amanda. John was from Rhode Island, Tom from Connecticut and Amanda from Massachusetts. We stayed in touch for a few months upon our releases.

John had been clean and sober for five years previous to relapsing back to a life of alcohol. This landed him in treatment where we were now together. He would be the one to drive many stakes through the center of my heart and soul within the thirty days that we were residents there. John knew what the insidiousness of this illness entailed. He also knew what the solution was, what was required of one who wishes to be truly free. And had the virtue of patience to watch, and wait. Wait for the perfect opportunity to drive those stakes into my delusions. He knew instinctively when and how from the time that he was sober previous to arriving.

I was institutionalized at the age of eighteen but thought I was in a country club. The breakfast, lunch and dinners that were served to us were pretty fabulous and it was like an all-you-can-eat buffet. The accommodations and surrounding treatments were far more comfortable than where I was used to living.

I grew to be a professional hi-lo jack player in my time there. I learned the fine skill of horseshoes and volleyball. I learned how to participate in that stream of life and how to wedge a fudgesicle in between your sheet and blanket on those hot summer New England days as a prank.

I learned how to eat again and even had a

romance while I was there. I read books and laid out in the sun and sometimes walked down to watch the busy traffic on route 1 from all of the people returning from the beach at the end of the day.

My sense of humor was fast to return as was my anger and rage that caused that initial separation from God. I would become part of the herd as we made our way to this session and that session. As we made our way to the cafeteria to eat and back to the units for additional group sessions. And then later back through those winding halls to this lecture or that talk.

During the week and on Saturday and Sunday nights we were filed into the cafeteria as some fellows from Alcoholics Anonymous came in to put on a meeting for us. I sat in these meetings somewhat aloof and uninterested. While I felt a sense of relief that I had been separated from the alcohol and drugs I was still waiting for the classes on how to control my drinking or the lectures on how to win at this game of life. Those classes or lectures were not on the agenda in this facility.

What they offered us was something called "Integrated Change Therapy" but the real thing we were being pushed to was the program of those twelve steps. I really didn't want anything to do with either no matter how they sugarcoated it. I would attend these meetings and watch the clock dreaming of kicking another patient's ass at a game of cards.

I sat in these meetings and everything that was said made no sense to me. They spoke about a sober life and steps and meetings and sponsors and groups and pigeons and this and that and this and that. Blah, blah, blah. They weren't reaching me as I wasn't reachable yet. My roommate John just waited, and watched.

The groups that came into the facility seemed to all have a different flavor about them. They had different approaches as many do today. I made sure that I wore a beer t-shirt to the meeting, making sure I sat within view of the speaker. I couldn't give them the finger or say "Fuck you" so the t-shirt would have to speak for me. I was the belligerent one.

One of these groups showed up on a trail of Harleys and they wore "colors." They were covered with ink and they looked pretty rough. You knew they were coming as you could hear the approach of their bikes long before they came into view. The name of their club was "The Fifth Chapter," named after the fifth chapter in the book titled *Alcoholics Anonymous*. They were a sober motorcycle club. This peaked my interest for about ten seconds. They visited twice a week to put on a meeting. And their stories were tragic. Far from what I had ever experienced while drinking.

For about three weeks I treated the place like Club Med. A playground for my own enjoyment. And then the magic and shift began.

Another patient close in age to me was deposited onto our unit. Up until this point I was by far the youngest one there. An observation that did not go unnoticed by me and only seemed to bolster my belief that I was different and not like the other patients there or like the visitors who brought these meetings in. They kept identifying themselves as "alcoholics" or "grateful alcoholics." I thought the latter of these must really be nuts to feel a sense of gratitude for this label that is steeped in stigma. I couldn't relate at any level. Once they said this I turned the volume off in my mind and was now just doing time for the hour and a half while the "blah, blah, blah" happened. I would begin dreaming of being free or back in that square of "the four of us."

The young patient who landed on our unit came in wearing a leather coat on a 90 degree day. That I can remember. John began his work with me when he arrived. He instinctively knew that if I got close to another young person this whole treatment thing might not stick to me. He pointed out that the music he listened to was somewhat evil-sounding. John didn't know what kind of music I listened to and that it gravitated to what amounted to be dark in theme, and lyrics.

At the same time this was happening the motorcycle club visited to bring us a meeting. I was starting to clear up a bit now; I was coming out of the fog of six years that alcohol and drugs wrapped me in. The colors were brighter, the smells more intoxicating. I went to the meeting with an expectation of being bored and was just following the crowd as we filed into the cafeteria.

A couple of the men spoke and I didn't listen to them. Then two men spoke and I experienced a shift that I still feel to this day over thirty years later when I recall this moment in my time there. It was that powerful and it would lead me to embrace a new way of life that was coming into view slowly.

"My name is Stubbs and I'm a drunk and a dope fiend" came the introduction from the man who was as wide as he was tall. "Stubbs."

I looked up from my hands that were doing battle with each other on the table top while I attempted to nod off. I thought to myself "What the hell did he just say?" with a moment of identification taking place somewhere in the depths of my being.

I dismissed this anomaly of thought as swiftly as it arrived. Denial can be rich. I settled into watching my hands wrestle with each other on the top of the table. I attempted to withdraw and go back into my trance I had become accustomed to in these meetings. And the dreams I had of the hot chick on the other unit. This was interrupted by clapping from everyone around me; the signal for me that he was finished speaking. I shifted in my seat to keep my ass from falling asleep.

"I'm a drunk and a junkie and they call me Animal" came the next line I heard when the clapping fell away. It was said by a man in the motorcycle club who looked as rough as the coarsest grit of sandpaper does. He was covered in ink and he wore jeans and a leather vest. And a goatee. His movements were calculated.

I heard this one loud and clear. And John was watching me. He was watching my reaction, and waiting.

I listened to this man and his "story." As I did I thought about the words Stubbs had used to identify himself and then the words Animal used to identify himself before they spoke to us. Up until this point everyone else was an "alcoholic" and I couldn't *relate* to that which put me in that comfortable position of dismissing them. "They didn't understand me" was what I perceived about them, and everyone else in the rehab and all those who visited. Including my family and friends who would arrive for visiting hours on Sundays. I felt misunderstood and alone even in the midst of a crowded room and now the alcohol and drugs were removed from me and that underlying cause for the start of it all, that first resentment I copped toward God began to bubble up within, and rise to the surface like bubbles in champagne rising to the top of a flute.

John just watched, and waited.

The way these men started their "talk" woke me up, somewhat. It roused me just enough to start thinking a bit differently. At this point I was there for three weeks. And in that time I did realize this was indeed not a drinking school nor was there any talk about controlling the drinking. This I gathered from the lectures.

I returned to the unit and John and I went into our room. There would be no playing of cards or television that night. Previous to this John had nearly convinced me that the other young patient was dark and evil. Without the alcohol and drugs to medicate my already twisted thinking and mind I would have believed anything I was told under the delusions that were in play.

John and I spoke for a bit about the meeting. I asked him the difference between a drunk and an alcoholic, between a dope fiend and a junkie and a drug addict. He answered these questions with a line of questions. Then the conversation turned to the "evil patient," and God. The God I now felt a fear of. I had a fear of His retribution. Like He would cast me into some hell for all that I had done, those damages caused by the alcohol and drugs and even the damages from a life lived selfishly before all of that. We didn't speak to this, at all. It's sort of understood between alcoholics and needs no words spoken.

John convinced me that maybe we should pray for the evil patient. I certainly agreed that *he* definitely needed help from God. I didn't know I needed God's help. John asked me to pray with him. I hesitantly agreed. Then John stood up.

"Where are you going?" I asked John.

"We are going to pray and it should be done on our knees."

"Okay." There was no turning back now, I had no choice.

We got down on our knees, he at his bed and me at mine. He said the words. I was too afraid to say anything. When I thought we were done praying for the fellow...

"Wait." John commanded.

I froze as this stunned me and then I looked at him. We remained on our knees as he spoke.

"Do you think we should ask God to remove the obsession to drink from us?"

"Sure, why not?" No turning back now I supposed.

He asked God to remove the obsession to drink or do drugs and then looked up at me.

"It's your turn now."

I repeated the exact words that John had said but there was something else mixed in there with the words. There was a desperation in there. My call to God was made in earnest, not just a fleeting "God please get me out of this I promise I won't do it again. I promise."

I haven't had the obsession to drink or do drugs since that very night. It was removed.

ROBERT ERNEST BACH

20 - FREEBIRD

I left the treatment facility a week or so later but before I left I enjoyed that shift in the last week by reaching out to others and again asking for help. John had waited for that one brief moment when perhaps something would click for me while in the treatment facility and when he recognized it he didn't hesitate. He seized that moment and opportunity to share with me what he knew from when he was clean and sober those five years. That the real solution he found to solving the problems for an alcoholic was God. He made it easy for me to approach this God even though I was filled with that fear.

I walked into that treatment center a desperate kid. And that desperation makes for a strong additive, a fuel to a willingness to do whatever is required to stay sober. That was a by-product of the prayer I mouthed to God. I became willing to do whatever had to be done to stay clean and sober. And besides when I was there a counselor announced to a room full of us as we gathered for a session that only one of us twenty were going to make it a full year clean and sober. I wanted to be that *one* and fully realized that I couldn't do this on my own, I would need help.

Animal and Stubbs showed up a couple of nights later with some of the other guys and put on a meeting. I was looking forward to seeing them and waited for the rumble of the Harleys to grow louder as they approached. I sat through the meeting and listened. I listened to every word, even from the ones that identified themselves as "alcoholics."

The thing about Animal and Stubbs, more to the point, the way they identified themselves a couple of nights before, was that I could relate to being a drunk. I could relate to being a junkie. I could relate to being a dope fiend. That was me. I stopped feeling alone in this battle right then and there.

John arrived a day after I did and was due to be released the day after me. I was due to get out on the 4th of July and he the 5th. I wanted to stay that extra day and was allowed to do so. John wanted to leave two days earlier but was told he couldn't leave. He had a flight and vacation planned for that date and wanted to go. Alcoholics pretty much do what they want before they've recovered so we said our good-byes the day he wasn't supposed to leave and later that night he snuck out of the sliding glass door in the kitchen with his packed bags. I was sad to see him go as he gave everything he had in him in that last week to fill me with the information I would need when I walked away from there.

The staff bid farewell to me, and I to them, on the morning of July 5th and I promised to return, not as a patient but as someone who would be willing to help out. I left with my bag packed and was able to purchase all of the literature I could from the bookstore before I left. When I left I felt alone, more alone than I've ever felt in my life up until this time.

I returned to my mother's house that day and there was no celebration for me, rightly so. Why should there be? My mother and sister were still pretty hurt by the way I treated them. I went into my bedroom and everything was as it was a month before. The holes were still in the walls. My bed was still unmade. My stuff was right where I left it and all of this kind of freaked me out. Doubt crept in and I had a choice to make. Fuck it and just pick up where I left off, begin drinking or drugging. Or find a meeting or another alcoholic to speak with. I chose the latter.

With that decision I set to cleaning up my bedroom and tossing all of the paraphernalia out that was still there. That was all the power I had in me to do. The ability to clean up my past and repair relationships I had burned was not in me yet. I went to a meeting that night, back at the facility I just left. It was a Saturday.

I went to a meeting around the corner from my house on the Tuesday and when I arrived there was one other man there. I explained that I was new and out of treatment. He looked at me through untrusting eyes that were wrapped in a wrinkled face and topped with white hair, he was old, and told me he spilled more booze than I ever drank. This was my first meeting out of treatment. (Welcome to Alcoholics Anonymous.) I attended that meeting out of spite for quite a while to stick it to that guy.

The next night I returned to High Point for a meeting as I missed the familiarity of the place, the safety of it and its surroundings. I was instantly relieved when I got there and saw that The Fifth Chapter club was there. I approached those two men after the meeting. It was the Wednesday after I left treatment. As my mind was now open to doing something about my problem all that was said in those first three weeks lost that fog that was wrapped around it like a tight hug. One of which was to "join a group." I was invited to join their group that met on Thursday nights and they told me they "had one spot left if I wanted to join." I told them I would see them the next night to take that last spot in the group if it was still open. I was relieved when they told me it was still open at that moment but that I should show up early.

The meeting began at 8pm and I arrived there sometime around six. With a willingness to take out the guy ahead of me in line if necessary with a few moves that were taught to me by a Vietnam vet in treatment. "Rip his ear clean off of his head if you want to stun him and rip his throat out if you want to kill him." (Welcome to Alcoholics Anonymous.)

Luckily for me and my sick mind there were no others before me in line and I was allowed to join the group. I was given a job that night and fell right into those open and welcoming arms. My first group believed it was their job to help people get sober and they began their job with this nut job, me, that night. It was the Good News Group and they proclaimed that the "good news" was that you didn't have to drink anymore.

While I was in treatment they spoke to a solution to the madness of the drink being along spiritual lines. The solution had to be on a basis of spirituality for the alcoholic, and altruism. I had that channel opened a crack the night John and I got on our knees and prayed together. It had been a couple of weeks since and that entire obsession was really gone. I found there was something to this God thing after all. My journey home to Him began once the alcohol and drugs were removed and I made the first move to *seek* Him. This was a beginning for me.

After the night John and I got on our knees together I recall speaking with my father on the payphone that was on the unit one evening. I told him that I had to look upon things spiritual and would need to follow this course as part of my treatment. At this time it was revealed to me just how deeply he was on his own search as he told me what they were looking at in the realm of spirituality.

I joined that first group and within a very short time considered myself lucky that I had the rudiments of faith handed to me while in treatment. Some of the other members were not so fortunate and the group had a remedy for solving this problem. The problem of fear surrounding God, the problem of all those real and *imagined* resentments that block that channel to Him.

They would take members up in a perfectly fine and working airplane and toss them out of it. They took these members sky diving and it was almost guaranteed that when their feet were planted back on the ground they had an inkling of God and His presence. There was no need for them to do this with me.

While I do believe today that God casts us here as spirits, an extension of Himself, and wraps us in meatsuits, I have come to believe that He is still there from the very start when we arrive. It's just that we, as humans, tend to get bounced around in that pinball machine of life, that human experience we all endure, and can get easily pulled away from Him. Some more so than others and still others not so much. It is when this happens that we have that freewill that is also installed in us, unlike every other creature or creation on Earth, that can get in our way and can ultimately separate us from Him through a decision, whether consciously or unconsciously. Maybe one day those freewills will be more tame with time and through human experiences and we will all come to know how to keep that connection throughout our entire lives.

I consider myself more than fortunate today, indeed blessed, for all of those experiences I had growing up as they resulted in a bottoming out of consciousness, a bottoming out of that freewill, that set me on a path back to God and I've been able to seek Him since I got sober. Many do not get to enjoy that process or can never break free from the detriments of the freewill that can so easily become misaligned and are doomed to wander aimlessly.

21 - A NEW SUIT

If I spent the time cataloging every year of my recovery I'm afraid you might beg to get off of the ride. I will reach into my memory and share a bit about my first year before I give you those "bullet points" that will deepen our relationship together though I may never have the opportunity to look into your eyes, those windows to the soul.

I spent all of my years up until the day I walked into that treatment facility working with all of the ideas, emotions, and attitudes that were so freely handed to me by my family and society. A great many of these would change instantly and lose their power, their grip, on me just by abstaining from the alcohol and drugs. And still a great many I would carry for most of my life until I had that spiritual upheaval that we will explore and try to define with words later on in the story.

As I became more sober in mind some of the ideas that I had instilled deep within became evident and were tossed aside easily. The delusions were recognized and seen as unfit for a sober life. The emotions that were born out of the delusions dissolved like a sugar cube in hot water and my attitude shifted, somewhat, by seeing many who were in worse shape than I in Alcoholics Anonymous meetings.

It would be years later, twenty-six, before I would see a line that would begin to explain the upheaval *after* I had it. The pioneers of AA spoke to their experience and put forth a pretty explosive proposition. They shared that just staying sober would hardly do the trick. They spoke to the alcohol as being the *surface* of the problem and that more work would be needed to fully recover.

The irony is that when I experienced these shifts of consciousness just by being sober I easily replaced them with different ideas, emotions, and attitudes. And most of these were handed to me in that first year of recovery by my group, by other groups, by other members of AA. And by experience I would gain.

I've described, albeit lightly, my first group. It was probably one of the toughest, no nonsense groups in Rhode Island at the time. Not warm and fuzzy, they did things differently. With color as vivid as the color of their patches and ink.

When an anniversary was celebrated it was likely a cake was going to be thrown across the room. Another member of the group wished to be a cowboy and he would wear 45's on his hips. One fellow dressed as a nun one night. They traveled to commitments to other groups in a hearse or an ambulance. I was eighteen years old, a puppy, in mind and spirit, and I loved it. It felt like there was no need to grow up. As this madness surrounded me I felt like I was home, at last. If I told another person in AA which group I belonged to it was met with raised eyebrows.

Perhaps now you see why I valued those kneecaps of mine, I feared for their delicacy and placement on my being. And when I was told "you'll go through the steps or we'll shoot your kneecaps off," it was believed. Maybe you *can* scare an alcoholic who is sober. Nah. Only for a blip of time.

The members of AA in my area didn't follow the directions the pioneers left us with their first piece of literature, the Big Book. There was another book my group used at the time published by Hazelden. The *method* was brought to us through Boston, Massachusetts after it made its way through, and down from, the penitentiary system in Canada. It was thought to be a quick mechanism of getting people through the steps.

We would gather at the church and begin these groups of men-only and women-only rooms in September and would be finished by the late spring the following year. I would go on to do these groups for the next twenty six years, starting as another person in the room, to chairing the meeting to ultimately administering the groups each year. After I hit the beginning of that spiritual upheaval that lasted three months I would walk away from them and see their compromised style. For twenty-six years they failed to produce what needed to happen, a full blown, five alarm spiritual experience.

That is not to say there wasn't value in this method and that I didn't get a glimpse of what true recovery was. In fact the first time I went through there was an effect for me. I was freed, to a limited extent, from that guilt, shame and remorse I carried into recovery from a life lived soaked in booze and strung out on drugs. To an extent. Did I have what they speak to in that twelfth step, a spiritual awakening? Well sort of.

I did continue to recognize that I was indeed without power when it came to the drink, the booze. I came to fully appreciate the first part of the first step when it speaks to the powerlessness over the alcohol. I got that. What I failed to see was the second part of step one where it speaks to the living an unmanageable life. I saw how my life became absolutely, without a question, unmanageable when it came to the excesses of alcohol and drugs and how *they* caused unmanageability. Tragically it would take twenty-six years before I would see that the pioneers were not just referencing the unmanageability as it relates to alcohol. Today I believe through my own experience and practice of those divine principles that it also refers, and maybe more importantly, to the unmanageability of my mind. My delusions. Those, dare I type it again?...ideas, emotions, and attitudes.

It may appear that I'm slipping the members of the first group I belonged to under the bus along with other people in AA and maybe to some extent I am. I was filled with new ideas very easily when I got sober. I was trying to relearn how to live life and deal with reality without the benefit of alcohol as a governor or barometer. I was like a new baby trying to walk for the first time and my legs were weak.

I was told that it would take a month for each year that I drank to recover, to get better. I was more of a basket case at six months than I was in the rehab. I was told to go to a meeting every day and if I couldn't get to a meeting that I should read some of the stories in the back of the Big Book as it would be "like going to a meeting." But stay away from the front of that book, "it will put you to sleep."

So, in reality, the idea formed was this...substitute meetings for the alcohol and drugs. The eventual message was switch your dependency to meetings. And I will submit this to you. If the meetings are made up of people, human beings, wasn't I in essence using these same people as a type of higher power? And aren't we as meatsuits fallible? This leaves a lot of room open for others in these meetings to play God, including me. I was told that if I had a problem defining who God is to look at Him as a "Group Of Drunks" and that eventually I would find His "Good Orderly Direction."

Perhaps you guessed it. I handed God the problem with the alcohol and drugs but held onto the rest. I continued to play God until eventually I nearly lost everything at twenty-six years of sobriety: my marriage, my children, my pets, my home, my business, and my life. I would have to lose my mind only to reclaim it. There were some really great moments in those twenty-six years but when they are laced with some downright nasty ones brought on by myself they became much like the fellowship of Alcoholics Anonymous. They, the great moments, became as feeble and depleted as the weakest moments. The fellowship will always be as strong as its weakest link. That may be my opinion yet do know that I offer it after being engrossed in it for thirty years. And I was one of its weakest links for many years.

Words are very powerful. They can inspire a

person or cut them to shreds. By either empowering or devouring. Perhaps you've been on the receiving end of someone's words that affected you in this manner.

For instance, when I began this journey into recovery a member told me that I "could do anything that I wanted to do in sobriety. If I wanted to be a thief, I could do this sober. If I wanted to cheat, I could do this sober. If I wanted to lie, I could do this sober too. *And that I would be better at it.*" He followed that tidbit of information with "as long as you can live with it."

As an alcoholic I lost my conscience while drinking. Remember I said I did the things I swore I would never do while out there. Just because the alcohol was no longer in the picture doesn't mean that a new conscience was reinstalled in me at the same time. I carried myself without a conscience for many, many years. I did not know the difference between right and wrong. My conscience, my barometer, had a broken needle. And when I was told that I can do anything I want as long as I stay sober and can live with it I pushed that envelope to the edge of the table and didn't bend down to pick it up when it went over the edge and fell on the floor. I just stepped on it, as a matter of fact, as it lay on the floor. Following rules and obeying laws was fine for you but I felt they didn't apply to me.

I was an unlovely creature when drinking and remained that way for quite some time in recovery. And this was easily overlooked as I could easily point to those around me in the halls of the meetings that I deemed sicker than myself. I had no moral compass and what was taught to me when I got sober didn't strike to the heart of the matter, that spiritual sickness and disconnect from God or the delusions that come to be a part of that disconnect. It would be years before my sound reasoning would be fully restored.

The one thing I wasn't told in that first year was that I could *recover*. Fully recover. Become *recovered*.

ROBERT ERNEST BACH

22 - INTERMEZZO NUMBER SIX

I attended Alcoholics Anonymous meetings for just over thirty years with the exception of one year. The year I took off was shortly after I was married the second time. My wife and I bought a home and were having a baby. I started working six days and four nights a week and she became a stay at home Mom. Eventually I returned to the meetings.

I joined many groups and was active in each of them. I even participated in starting groups, one because I didn't get my way at one of the groups. Most groups are formed for this reason.

After having that spiritual upheaval at twenty-six years of sobriety I became heavily involved with a group. A group of men and women who followed the process and directions as the pioneers had laid them out in that Big Book.

In addition I began to work with many men as part of that altruism that comes naturally with the awakening. I was to sit in a chair each Friday night at 6pm and lead a meeting, a meeting that served two purposes. One, to feed my ego. Two, to deepen my own understanding of these principles and what had happened to me as the result of following those directions. It was when I came to see the malignancy of that first purpose that I reached a decision to give up that chair in the back room and leave the group.

I became fascinated with the history of Alcoholics Anonymous, the founders and pioneers, and the *magic* they came upon that would bring an alcoholic, a spiritually deficient and sick individual, to a full recovery of their senses and mind. So much so that when I came upon some more intensely structured meetings I became enamored with them. I started some online research and found that the structure of these came to be in the 1980's, the same decade that I was freed from alcohol.

In my research and with some additional visits to meetings like this I decided I would like to start one. I asked five other men to be a part of it as I didn't want it to be "Bobby's meeting." This decision was made after speaking with one of those founding members of this structure, he in Canada, and his revealing to me the downfall(s) for this type of meeting. He simply shared that the downfall would be through the egos of the members. The unchecked pride and puffed up chests that were beat with the drum of arrogance after surviving the process and making it out the other side.

In just four short years I was to see that there was more to it than just surviving the process. It was by constantly trying to practice those principles and seeking God that I was able to break free from an *attachment* to the process. Maybe it was the depth of that spiritual experience that put me in that place. The place I enjoy today. The morning after I left the group(s) that became very comfortable for me but grew increasingly uncomfortable I woke to a decision to leave that heavily-structured meeting I was a part of starting as well.

I either left Alcoholics Anonymous or Alcoholics Anonymous left me. It was beginning to feel like a cult to me wrapped in spiritual disease everywhere I looked. If there is a downfall to being rocketed into a new existence and reborn with such dramatic effect it was this: I could see spiritual sickness all about me. That pointing the finger at others and knowing there are three pointing back? Well once you come to a full realization of your own deficiencies at such a grand scale, propelling you on a different course, it becomes easier to see spiritual sickness lurking just behind the facade of love and light.

The decision to leave the meetings and explore this new God-consciousness, to test it, has brought about many revelations which we are going to look at. After thirty years of a sick dependence on people, on meetings, or groups to keep me sober, and other dependencies that can be naturally formed while attending and participating in recovery meetings I was shown freedom from them. If the whole design of the process of recovery by the pioneers clearly points to becoming free of dependence and shifting that trust and reliance from people and things to God then I have achieved this, as was precisely predicted by them and even in the writings of one of the founding members years after this society was formed.

One of two things was going to happen when I left AA after thirty years. I was either going to backslide into unconsciousness and go off the rails or

I would enter a new chapter, a new room, that would hold the keys to my future relationship with my Maker, thereby creating a new usefulness to Him as one of his agents.

After my detox from the meetings and dependency on them my vision became clearer. The same type of fog that surrounded my mind while I was in treatment began to fade away when it came to the meetings and fellowship of AA. More delusions began to be smashed. The first two weeks seemed difficult yet I kept turning to God in everything. I began this as a forty day prayer challenge. It was simply an effort to unplug from social media, the news and even some people that became anchors or weights on my ankles. In my mind all I could hear was "Fly like an eagle." I believe it was after these two weeks that I was tossed out of bed violently at 3am and sat in that chair and heard "Write." And this is why I'm here with you.

If you're in recovery and no one has told you that you can fully recover yet, you can. If you are in recovery, no matter the program, and this has offended you, that's okay. Maybe it will inspire you to dig deeper. If you are the loved one of someone in recovery and you feel pushed aside I understand that. My wife felt the same way as you do.

I have come to know and have experienced freedom from dependencies and have been able to shift those unhealthy dependencies from people, places or things to God. And I must admit, it really isn't that difficult. It was a simple *decision*. And my decision was inspired by an *intuitive nudge*.

I still attend meetings but am not in the forefront, that spotlight, anymore. I sit at the rear of the bus now. I do not belong to a group nor do I have a sponsor. I haven't had a sponsor, someone to call every time I stub a toe, since that spiritual awakening, that reconnection to God. When I have its been in name only.

There is a line in the fifth chapter of the Big Book that reads "May you find Him now." When I first got sober I was told about the spiritual angle to recovery and encouraged to seek God. The problem is that with the number of delusions that served as an undercurrent to each of my thoughts and those colorful qualities that were born out of the ideas, emotions, and attitudes that created the guiding forces in my life, coupled with the suggestion that I could choose my own conception of God I created a sort of Franken-God. A God perceived in sick thought and created to serve me rather than I serving Him. And my Franken-God allowed for a latitude when it came to the set of morals and values I lived with for a long time sober. Loose and airy morals and values. Carefully crafted and designed by a still sick mind my Franken-God was only powerful enough to handle the problem I had with alcohol and drugs. I set out to try and live with my own power in all other areas. This ran contrary to what the founders intended with the words they set down for us.

ROBERT ERNEST BACH

23 - FRANKEN-GOD

I celebrated my first anniversary of sobriety with my group although there was a split and another group formed leaving us light by a few members. I really don't remember much of that first year at all. I went to a lot of meetings and did what everyone told me to do. I followed their directions and still no mention of the directions in that Big Book.

My life trudged on and I was able to get a job at a restaurant, quickly blasting through nearly every position from the front of the house to the back of the house. I always excelled at rising through the ranks and climbing that ladder. Eventually I was fired for stealing from that job, sober. I continued my relationship that was drenched in its own dysfunction with my high school sweetheart who I would eventually marry.

I tried to live as an adult with the emotions of a child in an adult world while acting like a child in adult scenes with childish perceptions. I felt like a square peg being jammed into a round hole. I felt out of place, and lost. I quickly began forming my Franken-God conception and constructing what I thought was His will for me. It fluctuated based on the people I was with, the level of my twisted needs at the moment, the situation or place I was in or whatever flavor of wind that was blowing thoughts through the storm in my mind. I was physically clean and sober yet was walking around with untreated alcoholism. The cause, that spiritual malady, was lurking beneath the surface.

While I was in treatment we were told we would need a higher power yet weren't told why we needed this. If we were I was not there for that lecture or session. Tom, one of the four in my square, really had a difficult time with this. We were told things like "choose your own conception," "make it a doorknob," and "as long as it's not you." Tom found a comic of The Family Circle with one of the kids walking, and holding a light bulb. The caption read "Look Mom, it's empty." We were told we could use a light bulb for a higher power! How a light bulb or a doorknob were going to keep me sober I do not know. Tom wrote in his own line below the caption. "But filling slowly." This would describe the painfully disconnected years that I would remain sober.

Apparently I must have convinced the group members that I was indeed going to stay sober as they began to call me "Bobby the Kid." While in treatment we were told we would need to get a sponsor. The man that became my sponsor was a member of my first group and I would come to know how sick he was. I was so naive and never saw it coming. I decided to move out of my mother's home and the easiest way to pull this off was to get an apartment that I could share with someone. My sponsor and I rented one from another fellow in the halls and we moved in together.

Two months later while sleeping and thinking I was having the coolest dream about sex I opened my eyes and saw my sponsor sitting aside the bed jerking me off. Talk about wanting a drink or drug to escape.

I cleared the bed six feet from the mattress and quickly showered. I felt like a piece of shit and dirty. I jumped in my car and drove into downtown Providence. As I looked about I saw the men sitting or sleeping on the benches, dirty and drunk, and wanted to feel their oblivion. Their seeming unconsciousness. I felt as dirty as they looked yet I remained sober.

In that first year I was walked through the twelve steps and felt a bit of relief from the storm within and the pulling of my past. I learned that even though I could make decisions on my own. most of them resulted in disaster. They would for years. I learned that the halls of Alcoholics Anonymous were filled with some really sick people, I one of them, all looking for the same thing. A God that would solve their problems yet no one that I was exposed to spoke to the directions the pioneers left behind. In hindsight it was like the blind leading the blind and I was blind and would attempt to lead the blind. Some of us practiced helping others get sober with those guys on the benches.

While it may appear I'm indicting Alcoholics Anonymous, and perhaps to a small extent I am, that is not my intent for sharing all of this. The principles they used were there long before the pioneers codified them for the alcoholic and have stood the test of time, decades. I'm sharing this as almost a sideline to the subject at hand with the hopes that many who wander those halls aimlessly might look for the authenticity of the actual program. I'm also well aware that I've lit a flame under a "cauldron of debate" but in a society so top heavy with inexperience perhaps it is the perfect time to light that fire.

What I didn't know about the insidiousness of this spiritual deficiency was that while I constructed this Franken-God in my mind it was the trick of the ego. They used to say the ego simply meant "Edging God Out." That was lost on me. Instead of having a total deflation of this ego and false pride when I got sober the exact opposite happened. I was spoken to like Al Franken did as his character Stuart Smalley on Saturday Night Live. My ego was massaged by those around me and this seemed to activate the massage therapist within, the storyteller that lived in that part of my mind that was delusional.

Through experience I was to find that the last thing an alcoholic needs is a massaging of their ego. What is most appropriate is a total leveling and grounding of that vile creature within. This is what I would experience years later. A serious deflation.

24 - PAPA DIED AND TOOK A PIECE OF ME WITH HIM

I slumbered though sixteen years of my life, sober, before Papa's spirit passed away, cancer. And I would still work with those guiding forces that were set up while growing up and through my drinking during this time.

I had tumultuous relationships one after the other and did marry that high school sweetheart. Out of this marriage a beautiful baby girl was born. That marriage would end circled in its own set of circumstances and battles that mirrored my parent's divorce.

I swore I would never marry again and I do believe God laughed at this as I indeed did get married again and am still married to a real trooper and peach. With this marriage came a beautiful daughter of hers who I look upon as my own.

I felt complete and with this I swore I wouldn't have any more children. I was happy with my "two little girls." My wife declared she wanted another baby and I don't think I spoke to her for a week and most likely told her I would withhold the fruit from her.

She won the argument and we have a son. I think God stood above the game board and probably had a great laugh at that one too. I was always trying to get my way.

I started businesses and lost businesses as a result of my character. I do not have the benefit of blaming these losses on circumstances outside of my power such as the economy.

I worked some pretty great jobs and some really crappy ones.

My wife and I bought a home and then another home. We built our lives together.

Everything seemed to be going pretty great for me right?

Yet there was still something amiss in me. I still felt like that square peg someone was trying to jam in the round hole. I felt incomplete, disconnected, and felt like I was trying to fake it until I made it. Made it to a place of peace and quiet. Made it to that place where I knew what I wanted to be when I grew up. I was still under the delusion that I could wrestle happiness out of life and I was always willing to go to any length to do so even if it meant I was going to hurt you or cause you pain. I was still searching, and yearning, for happiness. The effect of running you over in the process was a thought I easily dismissed.

If you looked at my physical life, the wife, the children, the family, the home, the business, the clothes, the cars, the pets, the physical trappings, the impression was that this kid really has his shit together. That couldn't have been further from the truth. Inside I was dying one day at a time. I've since worked with many men and women who have found themselves in that same position while sober.

Papa was a "rock" at this point. He was that wealth of information or counsel when I was at a total loss to solve a problem. When I got into trouble financially I would turn to him. I went to him with everything. And then he started getting sick.

By this time my ego had been well-massaged into an overinflated balloon that was near bursting. My mantra was "look what I did." Papa was diagnosed with cancer and my sister and I along with our spouses became his caretakers. We all stepped up and marched straight through the process of helping the cornerstone of our small family go home to God.

At the same time I had already been a member of a few groups in AA. I had a different sponsor, one who worked in the same industry as I and worked his own business out of the back of my shop. We were very close to one another. I was still "active" in AA and still didn't understand that *entire* idea of being "beyond human aid." I still, after all those years sober, believed that I actually held the power to control my own life and destiny. And I still put a lot of store in depending on others and things for my happiness and security, especially when I experienced a failure of my power.

Papa was the head of our family. He took care of all of us and when he died I lost another rock. I tried with all my might to step up and fill his shoes but to no avail. I was without the needed Power and Grounding to do so. This became a blow to my ego.

ROBERT ERNEST BACH

25 - TEN YEARS LOST

Papa died and his tribute was everything each of our veterans deserve. His funeral took place at the Veteran's Cemetery in RI and as it was finishing up the sun broke through the clouds. The collation took place at our home on my wife's birthday. As I watched everyone gather I was sinking deeper and deeper into despair that I tried to cover with my mask and ego. Tried.

I went on trudging though life day to day, went about trying to be the best husband and father that I could be. The best employer that I could be. The best friend that I could be.

I finished up one of those men's groups the spring after Papa died and it seemed the dust had settled a bit. I sat with my sponsor and attempted to empty all of the crap in my mind and heart through those twelve steps with the method I was still using. It only provided temporary relief until the storm within started to swirl its nastiness about my mind again.

Each time I approached and attempted to *go*

through the steps there was incremental progress made when it came to understanding the difference between my Franken-God and God. As I did some writing each year and shared what was written I would experience a bit more understanding. It did resemble the peeling of the layers of an onion and I did hit the actual core of my problem. I came upon that core issue with me and with alcoholics, the selfishness and self-centeredness and that the disconnect with God was indeed the result of that initial resentment toward him and resentments in general. What I didn't come upon was the knowledge of what was happening with me. Nor did my sponsor.

Allow me to preface the next part of the writing and what will be shared here with the following. I'm not a doctor. I'm not telling anyone what they should do or what course to take. This is my experience and further what I found to be a truth for me. And many others I have met since having these experiences.

From the first day I left treatment I was told the only time you take medication was under the supervision of a doctor. Aspirin only if your head was about to burst with pain. It was not looked upon kindly for alcoholics to be on medications for the mind. This is what I was taught when I got sober and I took it to be the *opinion* of AA.

What was to happen next as circumstances began to unfold led to what I have to say were the worst years of my life, the worst for my wife, for my children, for my mother, sister, her husband and their daughter, my employees and my friends. I was about to experience the real torturing that the mind can be subjected to. And I shared this madness freely. I was about to go back to a life of complete unconsciousness and taking others and holding them hostage would be one of the effects.

I woke up one morning and couldn't stand up, physically. I was doubled over in pain. I left the house and muscled through the day only to arrive at home later that night with the pain still there. I knew something was seriously wrong but didn't know what. I came to find out later, after that spiritual experience, that it was the revealing of my intuition, my sixth sense, and that it would have been an opportune time for the application of those twelve steps in the way they were left to us, more poignantly the original directions, recipe if you will. Although the method I used for years was insufficient to create a spiritual awakening over time they did reach into my center, or, more like my center was uncovered, like licks will uncover the center of a tootsie pop with some work.

Rather than get to a walk-in clinic or see a doctor I asked my wife to call my sponsor Gale. I knew this really wasn't a physical issue. I intuitively knew it had to do with God. I intuitively knew there was a solution to this and that it wasn't medical. I intuitively knew there was something spiritual about this issue I was having. I had come to believe by now that my intuition was directly tied to God. I knew that it, my intuition, was a barometer of sorts. Like knowing the difference between right and wrong.

I had made some progress over those sixteen years in having some of those old ideas, emotions, and attitudes shifted. I did eventually, in those sixteen years sober, come upon a set of morals and values I could live by comfortably and without much effort. I matured as I grew older. Isn't this what being a human being is all about?

I was about to walk away from that *moral compass* and didn't even know it. I was about to become angrier at God than I had been at a young age when I got my first resentment toward him. I was about to feel fear at a level never felt before. And I was to do this sober. But without a conscience as that would be squelched and eventually tucked in nicely and put to sleep. It became a ten year coma where I was present, at least physically, and would be able to witness and even remember everything when I finally woke up one morning begging God to please come get me and take me home. I was to become more *godless* than ever before in my life and the doctors would be more than happy to assist me, unknowingly, in this.

My sponsor arrived at my home and we all sat out on the deck in the back of the house. We spoke for quite some time trying to figure out what was happening with me and in my gut. I had spent countless hours of my life in shrink's offices, in therapist's office and even more in meetings of Alcoholics Anonymous always seeking to find the answers for my misalignment in life. Always searching and searching and searching. And just when I thought I had the answer and had it carefully scripted on that giant chalkboard of life it was erased. And then the search would begin again. I never minded this search as there were times that I was given a glimpse, here and there, and did feel some peace and quiet in my mind, and in my soul. Each glimpse came to me with a small package of hope that would always inspire me to keep moving forward and keep seeking those *Answers*.

As we sat there Gale revealed to me and my wife that he was on Paxil. A small dose to help with anxiety. This is something I never knew about him and he was sober a couple of years longer than I was. At this time I still placed a lot of value on *time* in sobriety and recovery. His *suggestion* was to see a doctor and see about going on medication. I placed so much trust and value in him as my sponsor as many of us are taught to do in Alcoholics Anonymous, as if he were a God, or was God. This was my own downfall for not having a honed conception of God and living a life with that well-massaged ego. I listened to him and went to the doctor.

I didn't go see a shrink. I went to my regular practitioner and explained everything that was happening and asked about medication for it. He was happy to prescribe for me and monitor it. He was well aware that I was clean and sober too. I always kept this up front with him over the years as different meds were needed for different regular situations. This began a period of ten years that would be lost, ending with that same exact doctor telling me that he misdiagnosed me after I went into his office at the end of it with a set of symptoms that dwarfed those I first presented him with.

I began taking a script for "anxiety." I now know it was untreated alcoholism, that spiritual malady, not anxiety. Though anxiety would likely be felt with spiritual sickness. Within a short time the anxiety seemed to subside and I *felt* better. And then it returned and as the doctor monitored this he would increase my dosage or change the script and at times two different scripts were taken. It became madness and my heart and soul became equally mad. I became bitter and angry. At one point I would go through the drive-through at the local CVS and write a check for 500$ and would do this the following month and the month following. Not only was it an emotional drain on my family it became a financial crusher too.

As I went along I could feel my God-consciousness, whatever I had gained of it over the years in recovery, slip away and with it those morals and values that came to me painfully through the small awakenings that I had come to embrace during my sixteen years sober.

Arguments began at home more often as I went back to trying to wear the God-shirt again. I tried to exercise my self-will and it always ended in a feeling of uselessness. I mentioned chapters ago, maybe the first or second, that my children have never seen me drink or do drugs. They may not have witnessed the madness that surrounded that time in my life but they were about to witness a father they never saw before. My wife a husband she had never seen before. And my mother and sister a son/brother they hadn't seen like this since he was a teenager in high school. My employees could only roll their eyes when I acted the madman. Ironically it is this experience in my life that really brings to life what those pioneers I keep referencing came upon. That the alcohol was a symptom of spiritual disconnect.

Now I could list all of the colorful and distasteful things that I did over this period of time but that would be fruitless for the purpose of this writing. Maybe a glimpse through your own life experience might help you to see it though. Think of the absolute worst thing you did with or without a conscious. Got it? Now imagine thinking about doing that or some version of that every day. Got it? Now imagine living in that same manner for close to ten years. It was pretty fucking ugly. Most of it was the storm in my mind yet some of it was acted upon and became reality.

I trudged on but in no time I was back to lying, cheating, and stealing. That is rather simple when you have no conscience to indicate the difference between right and wrong or the perception to know what is good and bad. In a short time I was passing on to my own children what was passed on to me in the way of those ideas, emotions, and attitudes. Some family members tried with what they had in them to point this out much like they did years before when I reached the end of the drinking. I didn't care and this pushed me farther away from them.

I began to live life by just going through the motion of it. I woke up and went to sleep. I continued to get on my knees in the morning and at night though I didn't *feel* a connection to God anymore. I continued to attend the AA meetings and even continued to work with others and administered those groups that began in the fall and ended in the spring. Whatever rules I had begun to follow, laws, were casually brushed aside and I began to believe they didn't apply to me. I grew numb. I grew aloof. I was slowly dying inside and began to feel lower and lower but had a fear about saying anything to anyone. Especially my sponsor.

Deep down inside I knew the medications were not working even though I followed the directions on the bottles. I felt helpless and hopeless at the same time but on some level I thought eventually they might start to work. That never came to be.

I just kept going. Isn't that all we can do at times?

During this time Gale's cancer returned and he began his next battle with it. Though I was sicker than I had ever been before I tried the best I could to be there for him. We did some pretty amazing things together in that last year, especially in our profession.

Gale died. Another of my rocks. And when he left I spiraled out of control. I felt an anger I never felt before. The day he died I asked one of my employees to bring a chainsaw to work with him and by the end of the day I was covered in sawdust and chain oil from cutting nearly every tree down that I could reach on the back of the property at the flower shop. If a staff member asked if I was okay I simply said "Yes, of course I am." I did this because the mask that had been tossed aside a few years prior had been picked back up and placed squarely on my face, my heart, and my soul. I was exactly where I was the day I walked into treatment at the age of eighteen yet now I was sober.

The loss of Gale was the beginning of the end for me. I began to withdraw and lost my zest for life and even my passion for floral and event design, something I absolutely fell in love with the first time I touched a flower years before. I tried with all of my power to reinvent myself but it didn't work. I began reading books and reviewing all I knew about those laws of attraction. No matter how much I studied and read, it seemed that those laws of nature were going to have their way with me no matter how much I resisted. I began to start losing.

I was losing my relationship with my wife and my daughters left our home as they were growing older. I was losing my relationship with my son, a relationship I always envisioned being the opposite of what my father and I had. My business began to slip and I had no direction. I became rudderless.

I remember a sunny day driving back to the flower shop down route 37 when I caught a glimpse of reality and thought I could hear something outside of my mind. It was something that came in the form of an answer. I was thinking about everything that was happening during a lucid moment when I felt a bit of clarity. A moment of Reason.

"God, why are you removing things from my life?" I thought out loud. There was no music playing in my truck.

I waited.

And I waited.

What came to me was this.

"You'll see."

As I began to experience loss at a time when money and things easily became a substitute for God, and faith in Him, I felt like I could get a handle on it. As if I could affect a change on my own without the help of anyone.

I picked up a book from the 1960's and began reading it and taking notes to try and redirect my mind, and the madness within. I was making great progress with my lessons and was feeling hopeful until I came upon a chapter that spoke to the corruption of the mind. It spoke to life never being a success until the mind is unfettered and the character of the individual right. At least this is the message I got from it. I threw the book across the room and screamed "I'm fucked!" I've read that title since and it was a mind-blower to drink in that part again.

With no other options at hand for me, at least in

my mind, my thoughts turned to checking out and taking my life, sober.

26 - INTERMEZZO NUMBER SEVEN

Once I had a spiritual experience that altered every aspect of my life, including my perception of God and His Power, the workings of my mind, and even my physical surroundings, I found that my feet were planted in a different soil. I became free of all the trappings about me and within me, that core problem that comes along with darkness and spiritual deficiency, the suffocating need to think only about myself. That transition and transformation was not had easily, it required effort. And the easiest method of understanding that darkness was by reaching out to others who were as sick as I was. I had to work with others to gain a deeper appreciation of what exactly really happened to me. It was their failure to go through the process that reminded me of that gratitude that became the undercurrent in my life that I live today. It was their awakenings and the raising of their own God-consciousness that allowed me to bear witness to God's Power. And most of all, working with others along with the explosive information revealed about myself when I went through those twelve steps the way I will describe to you led me to understand how effective my life can be for others. How valuable I can be to God as an agent to do His work when called out of His Dugout to do so. And those calls can come at any moment, anywhere, and at any time.

The greatest part of it all for me was the discovery that my spiritual awakening, more poignantly the experience leading up to it, through it and even afterward, came to match that of those pioneers. Not a close match. A 100 percent, the book they wrote decades ago explaining it, prediction filled, bona fide match.

Throughout the presentation of their experience as they lay out the instructions for someone with a spiritual disconnect to get reconnected they speak to a new usefulness that we will come upon. Futility will be cast aside with the same power that our defects of character will be. They speak to being reborn, the chance to begin life anew while never physically dying. And as we die, as we watch the old self and ego wither away, we are made fresh and live a purpose driven life. They speak to the fact that with this new position comes a perspective to be able to recognize the spiritually sick but more importantly the fact that the greatest part of this usefulness, this purpose, is that we are now qualified to be of use to those who wish to get better and be free. Not only have we been where that soul may be but we have endured the heavy lifting and are now on the other side of the work. Another dimension has been added to our lives with an understanding of what God's will is for us, an understanding that grows exponentially when you take the action with this new found freedom. The effect is life-changing, not only for the one being helped, but also for this new agent of God. The awakened one.

Neither Gale or I had this benefit about us. We did not have men or women in our lives who had this exact experience or if they were there neither one of us paid attention to them. Although deep in my intuition I knew my problem was not an anxiety issue or an issue of depression, that it was deeper, I had this incessant need to trust and rely on human beings rather than God. I couldn't let go so I took suggestions from people as the word of God. Never paying attention to humans as being fallible. I touched on that one earlier.

There was no way that Gale could've recognized what my problem was as he hadn't experienced the process of recovery as those pioneers had. He wasn't armed with the facts about the real nature of alcoholism, the spiritual malady.

Today I believe that not one human can understand me in the same manner that God does yet many come very close. Especially those who have suffered from a life disconnected from Him and are then reconnected back to Him. I can understand them as well. I am not only armed with the facts about my own spiritual dysfunction, and learn more each day, but I am aware of a solution that was able to heal the malady. I've recovered from that state of mind and body that was hopeless, as you will see, and can now be an agent of God's to help others do the same. Something no pill or doctor can do with a prescription. Those are outside agents, the agent must come from within. At least it had to for me and those pioneers.

I always looked at my life and thought that I had the fortune to live two lives in one. One filled with chaos and mayhem while I bounced around the pinball machine and then the other being a life without alcohol and drugs. I was astounded when I came out of that spiritual upheaval and began a new leg of that journey home to God. I quickly saw and understood that I was about to live an even newer life. A third life.

In the midst of the spiritual upheaval that would be the sweetest storm I'd experience in my life lasting roughly ninety days I walked around daily with tears in my eyes. It was pure bliss for me. My wife would look at me with skepticism and ask if I was okay. I answered that I was. She thought I was having a breakdown and on occasion asked if I wanted to go to the hospital. I knew she meant the mental hospital. It was that visible to those around me. The gentleman who acted as an agent of God and tour guide as I went through the process witnessed this and all he could do was laugh. He didn't have an experience as I had. It was that powerful, as powerful as what some of the pioneers experienced. Perhaps this is the reason why my own journey came to match those they wrote about decades before.

But before I came upon this shift, this casting out of ideas, emotions, and attitudes, this redirection of guiding forces, this new understanding of my relationship to God I needed to die again. The self would had to be leveled and the old me exorcised from my being. It, the ego, had to be ripped away from me with prying hands by God. And I had to ask Him to do this as I didn't have the power within to do it on my own. I had to surrender to Him completely and this is not always easy.

ROBERT ERNEST BACH

27 - THE END OF MY SECOND LIFE

As I close out the last chapters in Part Four and we make our way into that dark night of the soul I hope you haven't found the revealing story of my life, ambiguous as I have been with regard to minute details, in poor taste. To a great extent we are all storytellers, in our minds. It's like a separate part of us at times and can go way off course from our Center. Maybe this is why we are all lost to some extent. We don't expose our stories to the Light.

I've found that it is by leaving the present, the here and now, and going back that I become fully acquainted with those ideas, emotions, and attitudes. Sometimes we must go back in order to return to that present, that Gift. Revisiting our "stories," the lies we can tell ourselves, the work of the mind, the mind that gets bounced around that pinball machine, reveals a wealth of information so that we can recalibrate our inner compasses, setting us back on a stronger Path. The trick is to not get stuck there, or mugged.

At times I will return to that garden of good and evil to deepen my learning and understanding of what happened to be more effective in my life today. I have to leave the present only to return to it and most times it can come with some emotional tugs and there are still some thugs back there. I've found the benefit to be not only useful to living a spiritual life and to getting closer to God, but to serving others that would like to be free as well.

I grew very tired. And miserable. It was becoming increasingly obvious that the medications the doctor prescribed and his diagnosis were dead wrong. Although I was suffering the symptoms associated with an "anxiety disorder" and "depression," this was not the problem.

All I wanted to do was sleep and as everyone around me appeared to be enjoying life, participating in life, with a level of comfort that I was not, I tried to plaster that mask on my face but that mechanism kept dropping and revealing that something was seriously wrong with me. I had two Labradors and they came to work with me every day. I lost my ability to feel wonder and joy with these pets. I'm not sure but I think they lost interest in me too. Or maybe it was that overwhelming sense of self-pity completed by the failure in what I believed I was entitled to not coming to fruition.

I was toast. Well done burnt toast that couldn't be softened, at the moment.

My son was fourteen at the time and I would hear him ask my wife on more than one occasion "Why don't you divorce that fucking asshole?" But hey, I was sober right? That's enough isn't it?

I lost things in my life. My business, a huge part of my identity, slipped and the bank visited three times as they towed vehicles away as they were repossessed. My staff dwindled down from a harem of full timers to just one.

All I wanted to do was lay on the couch at the shop and if you looked at the outside appearance of the space it was apparent that something was amiss. I began to withdraw and give up a little more each day. The word recluse comes to mind at this moment.

My wife planned a trip to Puerto Rico, a solo trip. At the time our son and I would be staying home and she would travel with a family member and his husband. At about the same time I went to my doctor and explained what was going on. I didn't mention the daily thoughts of checking out, that suicidal tendency that was growing inside of me.

It was during this visit that he told me that he misdiagnosed me and thought that perhaps my issue was along the lines of ADD or ADHD. He recommended I seek help for this. My medications remained the same. At this time I was also eating pills for high cholesterol and high blood pressure.

I made the appointment for the ADD clinic and paid them a visit. Yes, I passed their battery of tests with flying colors and was handed a new diagnosis. It was suggested that I begin to take medications for ADHD. There was not one thing hyper about me, outside of my mind. I was sent to the other side of the clinic to meet with a shrink. To him, I carefully explained that I was clean and sober and this was met with a blank stare. I don't think he understood a thing about alcoholism, or recovery. Most times the idea of a body allergy and the peculiar mental twist is lost on doctors.

As we discussed different options for medication he explained that there were some medications that were non-habit forming. By this time I felt as if I lived by different alarms set throughout the day to remind me to take a medication for this or a medication for that.

In addition to adhering to the medications my doctor prescribed for anxiety and depression I now had to adhere to a new pill each day. It sucked. I mean really really sucked and all around me all I could see were those ugly trees. I felt as though my sanity was slipping away and that it was indeed time to check out.

I kept this regimen up and when the day came that I needed one of my scripts refilled I placed a call to my regular doctor to have him contact the pharmacy. I did not receive the return phone call, my wife did.

It was the doctor's wife, the nurse and office manager, who called my wife as she knew I would blow a fuse with what she was about to share. As my wife stood there and kept repeating "yes" and "okay" I knew she was speaking to the doctor's office. She hung up the telephone.

"All set? They're calling it in?" I demanded with zero patience.

"No."

"What!?! Why not!?!" I further demanded of her with a crazed look on my face that I can still feel the heat from while recalling this.

"There are two issues here." She said with all the patience and courage she could muster.

"Well?" Already defeated even more.

"First of all she explained that the dosage you have been taking exceeds the FDA guidelines. You're taking too much."

Not really giving a shit about this and only thinking about what I would be like without the medication I wanted to know the second part of it.

"And because you are now under the care of the ADD clinic they need to provide the prescriptions at this point."

She offered this last part with a look of "what the fuck is he going to do now, how is he going to react?"

I was actually remarkably calm and made a decision quickly. I was done taking the medications that were prescribed from my primary care doctor for the anxiety and depression. I knew it would take me at least eight weeks to get off of them and that I couldn't just drop them all in one shot. And that's exactly what I did. Under the primary's supervision I was weaned off of the medications and still visited the ADD clinic for check-ins and monitoring of what they were giving me.

I came off of the meds from the first doctor and that was a ride I wouldn't wish on anyone, or maybe I would. It was pretty scary and I grew paranoid. I withdrew even more if that was possible. As I came off of the medications reality began to set in. A reality that had been evaded for nearly ten years. My "rocks" were all gone now and consciousness began to creep back in. That core that I hit years before shortly after Papa died was exposed and it was a fit of screams and horror. This was now sitting beneath the surface of a new awareness of how I had been living a life of self-propulsion and the damages that I had caused in such a short period of time. I actually did more damage in that ten years without alcohol than I did in the six years while drinking. This added to my understanding that spiritual disease is a real thing. A nasty ego-driven malady. They should name a lot of those medications "Fuckitol."

I continued to fight on. I was still praying, getting on my knees in the morning and at night. Still going to the AA meetings. But I felt as though the will to fight was being lost by a sense that this world would be better off without me. My wife, my girls, my son, my pets, everyone would be better off without me. My sense of uselessness was deep, and it became reality.

I continued marching on. I continued to visit the ADD clinic and no, the medications were not working. After all that *wasn't* the problem. I would visit and be ushered into an RNP's office. She stared at her iPad and would ask me questions with zero eye contact.

"How's the medication?"

"It is not working."

"Do you want to increase the dose?"

"No."

"Let's increase the dose." And then: "See you in two weeks."

This went on for a couple of months and the conversation was the same each time. I could have told her I wanted oxy's or vic's and she would have said "Okay." After the non-habit forming medications were exhausted she tried the other ones. No result. Except for fits of rage and anger I hadn't felt since I was a teenager.

Fits of rage and anger so deep and powerful that when I tried to rip a door off of a kitchen cabinet while raging I sheered two fingertips off instead. I spent the night and the next day in the hospital and they couldn't be reattached. I am reminded of all that I have just shared with you each time I look at my hand.

On my last visit I had already decided that I was done with the treatments with her and the clinic. It was over. I was nearly at the point where I would surrender to God's mercy and even verbalized it during my last visit there. Maybe to try the words on to see if they could still fit or maybe a resignation that the only way out was to take my life. I felt as though the decision could be made for either as simply as the wind can shift its direction.

I was almost done.

I felt somewhat empowered that I was going to tell the RNP to screw. When I entered her office it was the same as all of the previous visits. Her face buried in the iPad with the same line of questions that seemed to be rehearsed and offered like an actor speaks their lines. It was my response that tore her face away from whatever her iPad was holding in the way of her attention.

"How's the medication?"

"It's   not   working.

"Do you want to increase the dose?"

"No. I'm all done taking the medications."

She looked up and asked: "What are you going to do?"

"I don't know, I'm going to leave it up to God."

There was no pleading on her part and she wished me the best. I left that office and never returned. I was now medication free and would unravel faster than ever before.

ROBERT ERNEST BACH

28 - MY SON SAVED ME

Growing up there was always a sense that I just didn't belong. Belong here on the planet or with anyone. Like a castaway. Casually tossed aside. Throughout my life I romanced the idea of not being here anymore. I didn't think of the effect on anyone around me, my family, my friends, teachers, or co-workers. I was too wrapped up in myself to extend my thoughts this far. I would always dream about taking myself out. My favorite dream was of a telephone pole in North Scituate, RI. It just happened to be placed in the center of an intersection with no island built around it and the lead up to it was a long straight away. I could get my mother's old Ford Comet up to 80 miles an hour before I would chicken out. I was even afraid to do this. I would go see this pole often and came to call it "Suicide Pole."

As I grew sicker and sicker in spirit and withdrew even deeper into despair and self-pity I would pick up a pistol and take the bullets out of the clip. I would dry fire the gun into my mouth and at the side of my head for practice. Still no thought of how this would affect those around me. None at all. It just wasn't there for me.

And then my son saved my life and didn't even know it. It was on a Sunday afternoon. This was preceded by a few circumstances that I came to see clearly. On the Tuesday previous to this I woke up in the morning with the dread that I was still alive. God had not fulfilled my wish to take my life while I slept the night before.

I woke to the thought "Another fucking day, you've gotta be kidding me?" As I lay there waiting for the absolute last moment before I had to rouse myself out of the bed with one eye on the clock and another on my thoughts I did some contemplating.

"If I don't shave this morning I can stay in bed for another five minutes." I thought. A thought I landed on each morning.

I listened to my wife downstairs as she was feeding the Labradors and talking to the cats, the zoo. Her voice was light and the television was on. She called upstairs to our son to get up and get in the shower. There was *life* in her voice. She was *alive*. "I don't want to be alive anymore." is what I thought.

Keep in mind that I was still praying in the morning and at night on my knees. I was still going to those meetings. I was still going through the motions as an empty shell filled with darkness that quickly extinguished light, especially yours if you came near me. "This is sobriety? This is the fruit of not drinking and going to AA meetings?"

"Maybe I would be better off just drinking or smoking a joint?"

As I watched these thoughts swirl down the

drain I began to cry. It was an uncontrollable sobbing and the tears were those big-ass splashy soupy ones. I was done. It was over.

I combat-rolled out of my bed and onto my knees. I closed my eyes as everything was blurry anyway and petitioned God with an earnestness not expressed since the first time I told my wife that I loved her. I was in so much pain and just wanted relief from being wrapped in my meatsuit.

"God. I'm begging you to please come and get me, please come take me home to You."

I never petitioned God like this before.

I got off of my knees and showered, I went to work. I was hoping He would send some angels by with a limousine and some flowers to pick me up. It never happened.

I've found that I can ask God in prayer for his favors but can't dictate the terms. He has those under wrap and it is up to me to look for the answer when it comes. And this is precisely what happened this week. I would be presented with *His Terms* and like faith, the way back to Him would be wrapped in mystery.

Two nights later I ventured out of the house to go to a meeting and to a group that I belonged to. A group that was out in the woods and a distance from my house. A group that wasn't that far from "Suicide Pole." I really didn't want to go but Something pushed from within and I responded to It.

When I arrived at the meeting I saw that another group was there to speak and put on a commitment for us. I was resentful toward one of their members and typically left a meeting when he was there. I wanted nothing to do with him. It was his group that would be speaking and I almost left until I saw that he was chairing and wouldn't be speaking. This I could accept. I poured a cup of coffee, grabbed some cookies and sat down. I had my arms folded tightly across my chest in that "Don't fuck with me or approach me!" stance. It was an effort for me to listen yet I muscled through. What was to happen in that space of one hour would lead to the answer that God provided to my prayer three days later on the Sunday as I drove with my son next to me in the passenger's seat of my truck.

Have you ever heard the story about the fellow sitting atop his home on the roof with the flood waters rising all around him, waters that are threatening to take his life? The one where he reaches out to God for help? He wants to be saved and doesn't want to die?

He prayed for help.

As the flood waters are rising faster and faster a fellow comes by in a hot air balloon and pleads with him to get in. He refuses, insisting he has a plan with God. A canoe slowly makes its way by the house and that fellow tells him to get in. He refuses and again insists that he has a plan with God. A little while later a motor boat comes up to the edge of the roof and this fellow asks him to get in to which he replies: "No, I have a plan with God." The motor boat leaves.

The flood waters rise and this man drowns. He arrives in heaven where he meets God. He asks God: "What happened? I thought You were coming to get me!" to which God replies "I sent a hot air balloon, a canoe and even a fast motor boat. You wouldn't jump in!"

The meeting I attended this Thursday night

became eerily similar to this story. Each speaker became a vessel sent from God with a very simple message. As each speaker talked about something I hadn't heard before in AA meetings in the twenty-six years I had been going to them I would label them in my mind. One was the hot air balloon. One the canoe, the other the motor boat. And for good measure there were more vehicles offered as well.

I felt a stirring from within. I felt a shift and would come to recognize this as the beginning of that spiritual experience that can resurrect a person. The spiritual experience that would breathe new life into me. Into my family and all those around me. It turned out to be one helluva painful journey but well worth it. But then again isn't anything worthy always balanced by the *necessary* work to achieve it?

By the end of the meeting I felt a touch of hope. And in the end the man I resented would speak too. It would be this man that I would reach out to just a few short hours after my son had a profound effect on me with just his presence, which turned out to be the finest present he will ever give to me.

I went home and went to sleep. I woke the next morning gripped with that same dread and within a day was practicing with an empty clip and gun. I woke on the Sunday morning, late, and finally had some coffee and took a shower. I had an appointment with my son at the cycle shop to have his bicycle tuned up at noon. We loaded his bike into my truck and made our way over to the East Bay. There were no words spoken between us as we drove. I killed "us." He sat in the passenger seat with his headphones on listening to his music and I, with my mask on, tried to act like a father. I'm confident it was painful, and confusing for him, as it was for me.

As I became more aware of the pain within me and the damage done my mind went back to the gun and the feeling of wanting to give up the fight. And then His presence and the presence of my son had a bearing on me, a sign, that could not be ignored. As we made the turn through the "Thurber's Avenue Curve" on the highway I looked at my son out of the corner of my eye. I looked upon a fourteen year old boy. I saw myself. I saw him. I saw the pain of my adolescence and could feel his pain.

"Who are you to be so selfish that you would want to check out and leave your son?"

"Who are you to do more harm in this lifetime?"

"Who are you to leave this little man, your work is not nearly finished yet?"

Those questions were asked at a level of volume that was cranked up pretty loud, it commanded my attention.

I saw this sign and recognized what had to be done, a phone call had to be made to ask for help. And this would require a swallowing of false pride and would signal the beginning of my third life. Another new beginning that would change every single aspect of my life and the lives of those around me.

I recognized that there was Something bigger than me at work here.

It was God.

PART FIVE

GOD-CONSCIOUSNESS

29 - OPENING THE DOORS

There are those in our lives who will jump in and help like no other can. I love the story about the man who is trapped in a deep hole on a busy sidewalk. He can't climb his way out and to all of the passers-by he pleads for help. Many souls walk by in their meatsuits and simply ignore him. He spots a doctor and yells for help and the doctor answers by taking out his prescription pad, jots a few lines and tears it off his pad. He tosses it into the hole and walks away. A short time later he sees a priest and calls to the father for assistance. The father kneels and says a prayer, makes the sign of the cross above him and stands up. He walks away. As he screams for help another man stops and looks down with compassion, with empathy. The man in the hole explains that he is stuck and needs assistance getting out. The compassionate soul jumps in the hole with the man.

The fellow in the hole looks at this man and asks: "How are we going to get out, we are both stuck down here now!?!" To which the fellow replies: "We will figure it out together!"

This is what became of the relationship between the man I resented and myself when I placed a call to him for help. On the Thursday night each of the speakers spoke to a solution that allowed them to fully recover from the spiritual malady and while they were doing this I became *aware* that this was indeed what my problem had been my entire life. They not only spoke to the solution they had found, they were clearly demonstrating it. It was evident in some of the tears they shed when speaking or the confidence when they spoke to the subject of God and His works that allowed them to be restored to sanity.

As the man I resented was the last to speak, and I had become somewhat settled by the end of the meeting, I listened to him. I was fully *open* at this point. In all the years sober and attending those meetings I had come to respect those who put together time, lengths of recovery. I've mentioned that it means zero to me now. As this man spoke he told a story of how he was sober twelve years when a man who was sober longer than twice that asked him to take him through the process of the twelve steps. It was at that moment that the ten years I had on this man became inconsequential. I learned that night that the length of recovery really held no weight when compared to the experience of those steps. More pointedly, the result of what can be if they are followed thoroughly as they were originally laid out by those pioneers. It was clear to me that each of the members that spoke that night, including the man I asked for help, were obviously armed with the facts about themselves and the solution. They were living proof of this result.

My son and I returned from our chore together and went separate ways when we entered our house. I laid on the couch in a fetal position and tried to watch some preseason football but couldn't concentrate on the game. It was impossible after *hearing* that loud voice while driving. My intuition kicked in with a light spark and I felt inspired to reach out to this man, the "mailman." I placed the call and it went to his voicemail. My delusional thinking led me to believe that he held me in contempt as I had he and he refused to answer the phone. I left a message and went back to my fetal position pulling "Nana" over me.

A short time later he returned my call. After a quick dispensing of small talk he asked me one question.

"What can I do for you?"

I asked him if he would take me through the steps, through the Big Book. There was silence on the other end of the phone and my mind quickly went to the thought that he had no desire to help. The pause and silence was one of the most excruciating periods of time I've experienced. This was followed by one statement.

"I'd be honored to."

The relief I felt was instantaneous and we made plans to meet two nights later at the flower shop where would meet over the next few weeks until he guided me into the heavy lifting required to recover.

To reconnect my conscience to God. To bring me home to God.

I would find out later that the silence was his tearful reaction to me asking for help.

30 - INTERMEZZO NUMBER EIGHT

"The aim of life is self-development. To realize one's nature perfectly - that is what each of us is here for." Oscar Wilde (1854-1900)

The process of those twelve steps is designed to do just this, and more. I was now to become fully acquainted with every aspect of my character. My nature. My constitution. I was now to become fully aware of every idea, emotion, and attitude that lurked beneath that mask that was laying on the floor at my feet.

It took many months and dare I say years, two or three, before I would start to understand those deep guiding forces and that storyteller within my mind, rigidly attached to an ego and pride that wanted nothing more than to survive this brutal beating. The ego attempted to claw its way to the surface intent on placing a new mask in the place where the other had been crushed. In fact the process of uncovering, recognizing, and understanding those guiding forces still takes place on a daily basis through the awareness of them and the ability to simply detach from my thinking.

The process began to snuff out that nasty selfishness and self-centeredness, the thinking that the world evolved around me and all was here for my pleasure. Replaced with a new awareness; the more solid idea that there is indeed a God and if He is my center, resentments and fears fall away from me. Thereby remaining unaffected by them. And free.

It was a bittersweet experience. Bitter in that it was painful, and sweet in that I would be set free from that *bondage of self*.

The quote by Oscar Wilde speaks to the aim of life. His quote may give the impression that it is the only aim. It is not. On the backside of that aim is the value I spoke to chapters ago and throughout the writing of becoming valuable to God as one of His agents. Of using the information that would be uncovered through the process to be able to help others become free and reconnect to God. A form of altruism that has not only benefitted God, and the other sufferer, but myself as well. It has been through working with others as was done with me that I have been able to not only enjoy a transformation of my spirit but have been able reclaim my relationship with God at a deeper and deeper level. This work continues today on so many levels with every person I cross paths with.

The pioneers of Alcoholics Anonymous codified their experience and put the process in an order to be easily understood in their first literary offering. The irony is that they didn't follow this process exactly, near as I can tell. They offered a rear-view vision of it as they stepped into a new God-consciousness and set to work helping others. They wrote the book in the past tense. This isn't the vehicle to get into the nitty gritty of the history but I bring this to the picture to make clear that even this seemed to be my experience as you will see. They didn't use those often referred to "twelve" steps. They had six that were taken, and adapted, from the religious movement called the Oxford Groups. When I look back on my experience it was more like those six steps. The understanding of the other steps that were added, what was their experience and mine, were the fruit of the work and awakenings.

The six steps were very simple and are as follows:

1. Complete deflation.
2. Dependence and guidance from a Higher Power.
3. Moral Inventory.
4. Confession.
5. Restitution.
6. Continued work with other alcoholics.

If any of these simple principles sound or feel familiar its most likely because they have been around for quite some time. Long before those Oxford Groups or even AA. There simplicity is divine. And they all work together; there is a synergy between all of them that seems to feed one another creating an amazing experience.

I believe that these principles will work for anyone willing to do the work to find their Center. And even that was predicted by the pioneers and even a good doctor who was there watching it all happen as these broken souls applied them to their lives and were repaired, restored.

Before I would enter this process of letting go of those old ideas, emotions, and attitudes I was already experiencing a bit of that "complete deflation." Before I began that writing process, that "moral inventory," that lasted 23 days averaging eight to ten hours a day, I had already begun with the idea that I had failed and that I would need "guidance." I sought this Power greater than I when I combat-rolled out of bed begging God to take me home. Before I began to formally make "restitution" I already started with my actions, my demonstration, fueled by a willingness to try something different. This demonstration was noticed by not only alcoholics in my life but by everyone around me. I was already beginning my work with others with this slight shift of "dependence" from the self to God. The "confession" served as an exorcism of sorts. A purging of the darkness from within and the exposure of it to the Light.

31 - TUESDAYS WITH "MAILMAN"

When I begged God to take me home I never imagined what the path would be like. It required all resentments and fears and harms, including sexual, to be fully examined. Oh yeah, it was brutal. And today I can easily see why many can't do it or fail to do it. It's as described in that first step from those Oxford Groups. It's a complete deflation of the self. A long-ass big drink of truth and when you think you've swallowed every drop the process continues as you make your way toward the Light through the necessary and easily pushed-aside work of seeking to make restitution, the process of making amends.

This path continued by meeting on Tuesday nights in the consultation room of the flower shop. This seemed safe to me as the shop had become an anchor in my life, a part of my *identity*. We met for five weeks or so and began to look at the experience of the pioneers. There were many revelations right from the first evening as we read. I was being exposed to a piece of literature that held no meaning to me.

I was dripping with desperation and hopelessness

and tried with all of my might to pay attention but that was clouded by the aforementioned. What I did have was a quality that would serve me well during the next three months. It was a willingness to do whatever had to be done to become free of resentment and fear.

At the sixth week I was growing extremely restless and all I wanted was peace from my mind and heart. I felt tortured without those medications that left me without a conscience for so long. The torment was harsh and if you've ever been taken off of those medications you know what I'm speaking of. I really can't tell you anything that was read or discussed during those six weeks. I couldn't focus.

The wreckage of my past and the effect it had on everyone around me was all I could see. Although I had turned my life over to God with that earnest prayer I still hadn't let go of my will absolutely. That didn't happen until I had a full taste of everything back there in the past, a full review.

As we made the approach to the writing part of my review we got on our knees together in what seemed to be somewhat of a ritual. It was a follow up to that first *real* prayer I offered to God weeks before.

In all the years that I lived after that initial disconnect I would reach out to God with those "foxhole prayers." Maybe you have done the same? You know the ones.

"God, if you get me out of this I swear I won't do it again."

"God please take this away."

"Insert your own here."

The element missing from all of those prayers said without passion to back them was any flash of willingness to match God's favor. There wasn't any spark in them for me and when they were said they were obstructed by resentment and fear, and me. My ego. My pride. It's difficult to petition God blocked by those things.

The third step of the program of Alcoholics Anonymous reads as follows:

"God, I offer myself to Thee---to build with me and to do with me as Thou wilt. Relieve me of the bondage of self, that I may better do Thy will. Take away my difficulties, that victory over them may bear witness to those I would help of Thy Power, Thy Love, and Thy Way of life. May I do Thy will always."[3]

This is the prayer I had been saying for years every morning on my knees but on the backside of that morning routine was a lack of willingness on my part to cooperate with it. I didn't grasp its full implication until well after I had a spiritual experience. Looking back now I wished it had come with a disclaimer of sorts. Something like "Strap yourself in, you're about to go for the Ride of a lifetime unlike any amusement ride you've experienced."

In essence I asked God to make me an agent of His. I asked Him to remove me from the picture, to empty me, so that I could be of value to Him. Although I wished to be relieved of the bondage of self, that darkness, I was not asking for my own benefit. On the contrary I was asking this of Him so that others might see a transformation, that they might bear witness to His Power and Love and Way. I

---

[3] See Bibliography

asked Him to create the scenario of overcoming difficulties through His Power so others may see His miracle. And this is exactly what happened to me. I came to find out that I didn't have the power to do this on my own. If I had had that power I never would have been in this situation in the first place. I wouldn't be here before my laptop typing this testimony..

In many ways when the two of us got off of our knees it felt like a prayer that went a bit farther than the initial one I offered weeks before. It was about four weeks before Thanksgiving in 2012 and on Thanksgiving morning I offered Him a prayer that served as the third and final prayer to seal a covenant with God. I became His fully to do with as He saw fit. That is when I began to really explore the real mystery of faith.

32 - A DISCONNECTED HUMAN NATURE

When I was growing up and in school I developed a lump on one of my fingers from writing and now being an adult of forty-four and already a slave to technological advances that lump had been long gone. The lump returned from a *hand-written* review of every aspect of my life and the interactions with each and every person throughout it. The review included a look at each *institution* I was involved with or exposed to. Be they different groups, associations, schools, foundations or the like. In addition I looked at different *principles* I bumped into along the way.

When we got up off of our knees after reciting that prayer, with earnestness, there was a sense of relief. There was a feeling of electricity in the room. That spirit of "I'm on my way" was felt inside deep within.

We returned to the table and I was given the part of the directions for a writing project that lasted for just over three weeks. This began with a cataloging of where I had been in my life and who was there and was broken down in five year increments. In hindsight it was like looking down a long hallway with doors to the left and to the right each holding hostage five years of my life. Some of these doors were covered with bright yellow "Do Not Cross" tape. Others were nailed shut. Still others were fortified with chains. The doors I wished never to open were rigged with hand grenades. There were rooms that I felt served no purpose outside of causing pain, and they were to be avoided at all costs. You have any of those back there?

There was pain and I didn't want to feel pain anymore. But this is exactly what had to be done for the process to be successful for me. I had to go into those rooms.

As I began the first part of the writing, the answering of that question "Where were you?," it was like removing those grenades and all of the yellow tape. It became an exercise in simply unlocking the doors to my past, my memories. I was cracking these doors open and letting in a bit of Light. I swear at times as they were opened I heard a hissing sound and saw smoke creep out through the crack.

As I continued the writing and made it to the second part of answering the next question of "Who was there?" difficulty presented itself. I now had to walk into these unlocked doors and look about the rooms. I began looking at these age groups and saw the almost natural expansion of life and then the retraction of it as I became sicker with the alcohol and drugs, the expansion again as I started in recovery, and the contraction again as I neared that ending with the pistol in my hand. I saw each person's face as I wrote their name down. I started to see the holes in my life with respect to family. As I jotted names down and their image came to my mind it would be wrapped in a whirlwind of feelings. Some did bring a smile to me but I found that for the better part each brought with them a storm of feelings and resentments that had long been tucked away deep within and evaded.

At the end of this long hallway was a Bright Light and deep within my being I knew I wasn't alone on this journey and that God was indeed there. I came to know that He was always there, just waiting for me to show up with humility and willingness.

As I entered each room, and brought with me His Light through prayer, these resentments swirling about in my mind, those "difficulties" referenced in that prayer, began to lose their power over me. Yet I was very far from seeing not only the ideas, emotions, and attitudes created within *and* my own failure in resolving them on my own. In addition, a clear look at just how *delusional* I became without His Power during all of those years lived selfishly.

My next course was to list each of the resentments I felt toward each of these faces, these people, whether family, friend, or foe. I listed each resentment I had against those institutions as well but wouldn't see the resentments held toward *principles* until I came out of the other end of the process.

It was relatively simple and easy to make a list of resentments. I had been nursing those nasty things my entire life, keeping them alive in case I needed their power and ammunition. Ammunition always at the ready for retaliation in the moments of war with family members. Looking at the areas of my life that became affected by them seemed to cut a bit deeper. It widened that fissure for God's Light to enter and do It's magic. I was flabbergasted at how even the smallest of resentments can permeate so many areas of one's life. The areas affected, but not limited to, my personal relationships, including sexual, and my self-esteem. To see how they created shifts in, and affected, my ambitions and financial security began to give me a glimpse into how our guiding forces can be redirected and refocused. Each of these resentments I came upon and uncovered clearly inspired all of the fears in my life and fueled their existence.

I've spent my entire life pointing my finger at others in contempt. I believe I have spoken about this. It's so easy to place blame on others. To hold someone else accountable for what is happening in our own lives rather than taking full responsibility for what became of our own choices. It's natural for all of us, alcoholic or non-alcoholic. It's human nature.

As I wrote and wrote, there were these *signs* that God was there. It felt like the entire process was divinely designed and that with each step throughout the day He was there. I had matched my prayer with a willingness to receive an answer and His Favor was shown to me. And at times it was comical.

I was self-employed at the time, still am, and had the freedom to create my own schedule when it came to my workload. My wife and I worked side by side, we still do, and she clearly understood what I was doing and what I needed to do. And given the husband and father that I had become I believe she welcomed any effort that might change me for the better. She picked up the slack for me in the flower shop and the design room. We arrived to work in the morning with our two Labradors dutifully in tow and worked on what needed to be done. As soon as this was accomplished I'd look up from my bench and look across to hers, she would look back at me. Sometimes she said "Go!" and at other times she expressed it with her eyes.

I always returned to my office to pound out more of the writing. This was how I was able to go for that non-stop, strap-your-seatbelt-on-ride with God. The deeper I got into the writing and the more I accomplished the more I wanted to do. I've found that there are two ways to do this process. You can either run through it or take your time. It's like taking a band-aid off. You either peel it back slowly or rip it off and get it over with. I wrote in a manner similar to the latter. What I've witnessed since is that those who tend to go for that slow approach don't reap the full benefit of what those pioneers found.

I'm not sure at which parts certain things happened but there were instances when *signs* became evident. One of them came as I was finishing up a part of the writing and left the office to stretch and call to get the directions for the next part of the writing. A mail truck pulled into the front parking lot. This was nothing new as I was now receiving certified mail from every Tom, Dick and Harry everyday as my life on the outside experienced a necessary crumbling to match my insides. Out came the mailman but this one wasn't carrying those familiar green slips. It was the mailman who began as my tour guide and he showed up at the exact moment I was about to call him to get the next part of the directions. This happened a couple of times. The surreal thing is that I came to hate the mailman for always bringing those green slips to be signed yet another one always brought hope.

I asked God and He always answered.

The first, second and third part of the writing brought with it tears and even some smiles as my memory was tossed about. Tossed and shaken like a carpet to remove the crumbs and dust. It was relatively easy up until this point and the real test of my meddle was about to begin.

The next part of the directions required that my hand that held that finger pointing at others be turned over and the three fingers pointing back at me be looked at. I had to shift away from that swamp of contempt and take a look at my part. My failure at trying to get my own way, at trying to wrestle happiness or satisfaction out of life, my failure at trying to run the show. I came to see just how delusional my mind had become with all of the stories I told myself. The stories about you and me. The lies about you and me. All born out of resentment. I came to see just how damaging a resentment can be, not only to my relationship with God, but to my mind. I was about to see how they served as a twisted nourishment to an ego that loves to eat that crap.

I was to answer a series of questions for each resentment I had. It was through the answering of these questions that I not only became awakened and aware of a resentment's destructive power but also to how sick they made me, spiritually, mentally, and physically. It was this part of the writing that brought about a spirit of forgiveness and compassion I never felt before. It was through my seeking of God and enlightenment of what kept me from Him that He allowed me to see just how sick I'd been and just how sick others can be as well. It was powerful and at times overwhelming. The more powerful and overwhelming it became the more my ego would tell me to scrap the effort, toss it into the fireplace and go back to a life of unconsciousness. The more powerful and overwhelming it became the more I would speak with God thereby deepening a fast-forming relationship with Him. The faster I wrote and the more hours I spent at it I had no choice but to rip the band-aid even quicker. I came to find out that I didn't have the luxury of pulling band-aids off slowly or even the luxury of feeling or entertaining resentments. Ironically it was through the writing that I learned how to gain mastery over these resentments, and any that would crop up in the future.

The questions that tore away and began shredding that muscle, the ego, that nourished my selfishness and self-centeredness were as follows:

"What did I want?" I had to write how I was *selfish*. That whole what's-in-it-for-me part that *had* to be exposed.

"What was the lie I told myself?" And "Was it the truth?" This first question struck to the heart of the dishonesty in my life. Most times the second question was answered with a "No" that seemed to echo throughout my being, cutting right to the delusional nature of my thinking. It chipped away at the storyteller that I had become, the storyteller that spun tales for you and fed my ego.

"What was the action I took?" This question struck to the center of that person that seeks only to satisfy himself. And most times the actions I took became colorful and had an undercurrent of retaliation to them for not getting my way.

And lastly,

"What was I afraid of?" The answering of this last question led to the next part of the writing that would be a full examination of my fears and these wouldn't be those typical "fear of flying" or "fear of heights" that many people carry. They would expose the deep-rooted fears born out of that disconnect with God.

The most difficult resentments to list were those I had against God and even myself. The resentments against myself were the harms that I had done to others but as I was writing and did not yet have a conscience and was to some extent ruled by that dark cloud I was told to list those as harms and *treat* them with those exacting questions. This writing came about later as you will see.

Try one on for size and see what you come up with. Take a resentment you have and ask yourself what areas of your life were hurt, threatened or interfered with. Your self-esteem, personal relationships, your pocketbook, your ambition, your sex relations, your fear? That was the easy part for me.

Now try banging that information against those questions. When I did this part, the answering of the questions, it wasn't done topically. There was some serious thought to it and most times it felt as though God fed me the answers much like He seems to be pushing my fingertips across the keyboard right now. After all, I had asked Him to remove my difficulties so that others might see His Work.

As I wrote and wrote and it seemed like it would never end I pushed forth and watched the lump on my finger gain size and strength. I also felt as though

God were doing all of the work for me. Like faith can be a mystery, what I just shared with you became mysterious as well. As much as I would like to put what was happening to me into words they will fall short in their description. Most times it is difficult to explain that spiritual experience, or moments within, which is why I love that prayer. It asks that God make it visible, something that can be witnessed to be believed rather than spoken to. As I wrote and wrote I felt a new Power coming forth from *within* that is equally difficult to explain yet as I felt this Power I felt inspired to redouble my already fast-paced efforts.

I wanted to be at one with God now and could already feel His presence, and His healing power. I felt myself being restored to sanity as each delusion was being smashed. I felt a new lightness about me and started to feel free for the first time in years from that bondage of self. I felt victory was around the corner. The old me was now being put to death and a new me was emerging. I *was* being reborn.

There are three parts to the writing process and the next would be the reconciliation of all the fears I uncovered in the last question answered. When I first approached the writing and was told I would be writing on fear I was quick to deny even having them. But when you are broken down in the manner that these pioneers came upon they are certainly uncovered. This is the brilliance of the directions they left us. The brilliance in clearing out that direct channel we each have to our Maker that get clogs with debris that blocks out the Light, and His grace.

ROBERT ERNEST BACH

33 - FALSE EVIDENCE APPEARING REAL

The writing process that uncovered the fears that became a part of my nature were pretty explosive to me. It was a shift that was unexpected. I didn't anticipate finding these and the brilliance of the writing process is that one is led directly to them. I had lived so many years on those medications that they were kept at bay and weren't felt or recognized. While there was a long list of fears it really came down to just two as a common denominator in my life and they fed those guiding forces. They became a source of power for them. They inspired nearly every decision throughout my life and only served to suck up any happiness or joy that might be felt, expressed or enjoyed. They were a set of masked bandits and took from me whatever they wished to ensure their own survival deep within.

In addition they fed the form of that God-shirt I always tried to wear and fill with my ego, the lower self. At their rawest form they came down to the "fear of not getting what I wanted" and the "fear of losing what I already had." It was through the writing on these that I uncovered just how deeply I relied on myself to keep them from being recognized, by you and by me. They inspired some of the craziest decisions I made in my life which always led to dismal circumstances, leading still further to my troubles. Fear was a nasty element in that disconnect from God. I was shown the true failure in my power with this part of the writing and was offered another choice. Either continue a self-willed, self-propelled existence of trusting and relying on myself or shift my trust and reliance to God. As I was so disconnected from God this was not an easy choice for me yet as I went further into the writing I became convinced of the uselessness of trying to live life on my own power. I became convinced that I needed a new Power and a relationship with that Power. I learned that an ego-driven life leads only to futility.

The irony is that once I recognized that I had these fears and began to appreciate their destructive power they were placed before me squarely to be experienced at their deepest. Again I was given a choice each time one of these fears surfaced from within my heart and mind. I could either run from the fear and try to bury it or I could turn to God and ask Him to remove it. I had no choice, I had to turn to God. The choice for me to do this was inspired by that decision I made to beg God to take me home, that decision I made when I began to walk the path He set me on and the prayer I said with the mailman.

After completing the writing I covered in the last chapter my effort reached a fever pitch. I couldn't stop writing and spent every waking moment at a table, desk or the kitchen counter watching the words flow from my pen. My effort increased as I went further beneath the surface of unconsciousness and as I did so the Light would shine brighter and the brighter the Light the more time I spent writing. My desperation to be free deepened instead of waning.

The uncovering of the destructive power fear had in my life was done by following this outline:

"List the fear." I simply listed the fear from the last part of the writing that was completed.

"Explain the fear." I wrote a brief description of the first time I felt it and the circumstances surrounding it. This is one of those places where I was to see those guiding forces and how they worked.

"How did I rely on myself?" The cleverness in answering this question served to uncover the fact that I indeed became a failure at trying to run the show and play God. Answering this question tied directly into the idea of complete deflation of the ego and pride. A false pride.

The next part might seem hokey and even childish like the teacher that makes you write "I will not pull Suzie Q's ponytails on the chalkboard" 50 times yet when you're in the midst of that self-exploration and are experiencing your own collegiate education about those guiding forces that you've lived by there is a profound resonance in the physical act of writing these lines over and over and over. I was to write these lines after the three preceding pieces were addressed. In essence I was back in school and was being reeducated. I was being shown how to gain mastery not only over resentments but over fear as well. Not only those fears in that dark and murky past but those that would surface in the coming days and months as many would come up, trying to invade and conquer my journey home to God.

They were:

"I should have trusted and relied on God."

And

"I ask God to remove my fear and direct my attention to what He would have me be."

An admission of my own failure and a simple redirection of the mind and heart. A redirection to God. Another prayer, a petition.

There was one more part of the writing and as I approached this I thought it would be the easiest part and that I would breeze through it unscathed and unharmed. I was delusional to believe this as this part of the process would serve as some of the nails in the coffin that carried my old self away. An old self that I would never be able to return to. It would be nearly impossible to try to put that mask on again after this spiritual experience. Impossible as once one's heart and mind experience a violent revolution of realizations at this depth that same person will do whatever is necessary to keep a new found God-consciousness no matter the cost or sacrifice needed to do so.

34 - THE BIRDS AND THE BEES

There is something about sex that brings out the best in human beings. And the worst. Some find it an easy subject to broach while still others have difficulty with it. Years ago when I belonged to that first group we would meet on Thursday nights and at certain times our meeting was cancelled as the church needed the space downstairs. We never seemed to get the cancellation into the announcements on time. I showed up one of these nights to stand outside and let everyone know that there was no meeting.

As people showed up and it became obvious the church was not using the space some of us decided to go forward with a meeting. We opened the doors and the room filled with about forty of us. We decided to have what is known as a discussion meeting. One of us would chair the meeting, he would share his story, and then choose a topic for the discussion portion of the meeting.

The gentleman who chaired the meeting was "Black Reggie." Remember this society is partly grounded in a spirit of anonymity which precludes us from using our last names openly in public and somehow this has filtered into the meetings, hence different "labels." Reggie was a lean black man who was a real spitfire. I would attend meetings with him and he would point to different fellows and could recognize whether they had *recovered* or were still asleep. It used to piss me off something awful when he did this. He would point to one and whisper to me "recovered," and still others and whisper "sick." He was usually right on the money with his calls, this is what happens when you do recover from that spiritual malady. You can *see* the ones who have recovered that relationship with their God and have had their sound reasoning restored. And you can see those who have not. I failed to recognize what he was trying to show and tell me. I failed to see this sign.

Reggie spoke for a bit and then opened the meeting for discussion and as a topic he chose sex. Half of the people in the room immediately got up and walked out the door. Those who stayed benefitted from a spirited discussion that many are loath to have. Sometimes it's a subject that is difficult to have, like it's dirty and the words will create scars or will burn us. Yet the pioneers dropped it in midst of the writing process and as one who endured it there is extreme value in exploring this part of our lives, and thinking.

The course of this part of the writing was as follows for me. I was to create yet another list of those who I had sex with. Pretty simple. This included everyone. Man, women, child and/or object. Thinking I was clean in this area I walked into it with a spirit of relief and as I knew I was nearing the end of the writing I was all the more desperate to just get it over with. I accomplished it in one day and don't believe I accomplished a thing at work that day. It was a Friday.

This part of the writing involved answering a line of questions surrounding each relationship, sexual encounter. And they were as follows:

"Who was the person or object?" I was instructed to write a few lines about this person or object.

"How was I selfish?" I had to answer how I selfishly used sex in this interaction. By the time I reached this part of the writing I had no difficulty in identifying my selfishness in any area of my life.

"How was I dishonest?" I had to identify what form of deception was involved in this interaction, if any at all.

"How was I inconsiderate?" By the time I landed in this third part of the writing process it was rather easy to see how I had been inconsiderate to so many people throughout my life. This part was easily written about, although painful.

"Who did I hurt?" This fifth question was the one that struck to the heart of the matter for me. It was the one that further uncovered the damages of a life lived selfishly.

"Who did I arouse jealousy in?" Typically there was another that I created this most human feeling in.

"Who did I arouse bitterness in?" Part of me would put forth a sarcastic chuckle as I read this question as it was clear that I stimulated bitterness in nearly everyone while living a disconnected and ungodly life.

"Who did I arouse suspicion in?" The question that sought to show me how my actions had that ripple effect on those involved.

"Where was I at fault?" The details involved in this answer shot right to the matter of living a life of trusting and relying on instincts that always seemed to be at odds with one another, always colliding and causing damage.

"What should I have done instead?" The most natural answer to this might have been that I should have trusted and relied on God but that was the easy way of answering this question. The answer I wrote was now directly related to that new spark of God-consciousness that was quickly coming from deep within and making its way to the surface to replace the mask that had fallen off.

I remember being in the living room of my home with my wife, she on the couch and I in the chair, and finishing this part of the writing. I finished and told her that it was now complete and that I could move on to the next part, the *confession*. I was relieved and looked at the totality of the notebooks with all of my writing and felt a great sense of accomplishment. This was tempered by an overwhelming sense of wonder at the depth of damages I had done living that life of self-propulsion. Frankly, I had been drilled into the ground by the process and I wasn't near done with it, there was so much more that needed to be done.

I took up my Blackberry and shot a text to the mailman exclaiming with great pride that I was finished and wanted to move on. He didn't return a text to me, he called. I made the assumption that I was done but he informed me that there was still one more part that needed to be written to which I replied something like "You are fucking kidding me right? I can't take this anymore!!!"

He quickly offered to me that it was just a small part and would be over with quickly.

The very last portion was a simple description of what I thought my ideal relationship should be based on all that I had uncovered with all three parts of the writing. I don't think I heard him say "good-bye" to me as I was already back in my chair in a flash. I returned the call to him in a half hour or so and announced yet again that I was finished.

The writing, and brilliance of it, exposed every minute detail of my life, my deficiencies and my flaws. It was painful and it was brutal. It was an endurance race and I can see clearly how so many who begin falter from it. In reality the truth about any situation can cut like a knife, especially when it comes to the truth about ourselves. It can be easier to live a life of oblivion always seeking to bury the truth through wishful thinking and the stories we make up in our minds, the lies we tell ourselves.

My life became a 55 gallon barrel filled with crap. It became messy and uncomfortable. And I tried with all of my own might to seal this barrel and hide its contents through every avenue possible whether it was the alcohol or drugs, through money, through sex, even foods and sugars, things and possessions, but when all of those failed to disguise the distaste within that barrel and no other barrel was to be had to start filling with more pain and it began to spill all over the place I had to empty the only one I had. And everything had to go.

The writing process began by cracking the lid and then removing it. Then looking into it from the outside and then stirring it up. I then had to get into that barrel and feel everything about it. I had to begin emptying that barrel so that room could made for some new stuff to be added. I needed new ideas, emotions, and attitudes to be placed within to help guide me. And that guidance would have to come from God through my newly recovered, and infantile, intuition. That sixth sense.

I had now walked down that hallway of my life and had paid a visit to each time period there. I walked into all of those rooms and did a thorough house cleaning in each of them. That Light at the end of the hall continued to shine and as I kept up the cleaning I was able to open the drapes in each of those rooms and let the Light filter in to every deep dark corner and crevice.

35 - INTERMEZZO NUMBER NINE

I'm not a scholar by any means, I have a high school equivalency certificate. I can't cite the Bible by verse, I'm not religiously educated nor am I overly familiar with religions. They just never did anything for me I guess yet there are some things about them that are attractive to me. Maybe it's a yearning from within to apply their principles, to be a better person. The act of confession as far as I can tell seems to be a part of many religions, at least this is what I perceive. And that to me is the most unattractive principle. Who wants to divulge the meat of the deep recesses of the mind and heart. Shit, you might be judged right?

When I was a child I was brought to church and shown "God's house." And then there were times when we visited His other houses. In my twisted little mind I recall being impressed that He had so many houses. And they were beautiful. I loved the colored windows! I was also brought to catechism classes each week by my mother. Nana insisted on this. These classes became a part of my life after that initial resentment toward God and that disconnect from Him. My own fall from His grace.

I remember days when my sister and I walked through the front door of the church school and walked straight down the hall past the office with the ladies sporting their white hair and proceeded out the side door. We blew off the class and went to the little drug store around the corner where they sold that penny candy. I didn't steal candy from this store as it was behind the glass in a cabinet although I was already a belligerent child and well on my way to self-destruction. I must have been seven years old and in the second grade.

It was about this time in those after-school-why-do-I-have-to-be-here-classes that I was told that I would be making my first confession, with our parish priest. I remember having that dog-shitting-razor-blades feeling about this. I was only a short time into a life of turning my back on God and do believe now as I look back that I was already filled with fear. This prospect of discussing my wrongs with another person terrified me. As if I would be caught disobeying God and would be reprimanded by Him, or worse, the priest. They seemed so powerful through my seven year old eyes and in my seven year old mind.

And then as we were being prepared for this chore in our classes the teacher offered this.

"If you are having difficulty coming up with anything ask the priest for help." This is what I heard and I have no doubt that this is what was said though maybe not with those exact words. I felt relief. I knew I could pull one over on the priest. Already looking for the easier and softer way, how very human of me. Already looking to absolve myself of responsibility, yet wanting the awesome responsibility of playing

God.

We were dressed in our little robes and one by one escorted into a side room, alone with the priest. I walked in feeling like Linda Blair in The Exorcist, like I would burn or something. I had plenty to confess already at that age. I had already turned into a liar, a cheat, and a thief yet there was no way I was going to give any of this information up to a complete stranger, never mind a priest.

As I entered this chamber I already had my plan formed in my mind. I would act the part of ignorance and ask this priest for help in identifying my wrongs. It worked splendidly and I was set free. I don't recall what the penance was for my wrongs but when he asked if I fought with my sister I could agree with that one. That was my sin. What an augury though, we've fought our entire lives.

When the pioneers offered their book of experiences they included that interaction between Dr. Jung and another fellow where the doctor defined that spiritual experience. I typed this line in this writing for you and in the midst of this line it speaks to having ideas, emotions, and attitudes *cast aside*. He used the word "suddenly" when referencing this. Not a gradual over time casting or tossing aside. To me that word suddenly implies abruptly, swiftly, like it has to happen quickly. Like the window of opportunity is minuscule and needs to be taken advantage of, and fast.

This became my exact experience once I was finished with my *confession*. Confession being one of those six principles that were followed by these pioneers. As much as I learned in the way of information through the writing about those guiding forces and as much as each of those rooms were drenched in God's Light it wasn't enough. It wasn't enough to crush that ego and pride, to reduce that selfishness and self-centeredness. I had no choice but to speak to and speak every word that was written in that catalog, the inventory that was taken of my life. My ideas, my emotions, and my attitudes. I had to do a confession nearly thirty-seven years after bamboozling a priest.

I had to admit not only to God and myself the exact *nature* of my wrongs, I had to admit these objectionable things about my constitution to another man. This took place the week of Thanksgiving 2012 and lasted for fifteen hours over three nights time. We began on the Sunday night, two nights after I completed the writing.

36 - THE EXORCIST

The mailman and I returned to the flower shop on a Sunday night to begin my confession and I was a bit fearful to share all of the nuances and details about that mask that I had been wearing my entire life. Of course I didn't know what to expect either. Like that mystery of faith, I didn't have a clue. I had done some of these confessions over the years while attending the AA meetings yet nothing to this extent. It was Thanksgiving week and of course the mailmen are busy. It's the week leading up to "Black Friday" and he would be out there in the cold all week working his ass off.

I simply read what was written down. It's just that easy of a process when it comes to what needs to be said. The uneasy part would be the revealing of so many long-hidden aspects of my life. Never had I bared so much of myself to anyone before. It took an hour or so before I found my stride and from there the reading of the content began to fall out easily.

As we wrapped up the first night he had a look on his face. It was not one of those "you did a great job" looks either. When I asked what the look was for he explained that I hadn't included my *harms* done to others. I was crushed. I didn't know what to say. Or do. I felt as though I failed. Days and weeks of fighting my way through the writing and I missed the mark. He explained the part that I missed and I made a note in my mind that I would never make the mistake of not being clear in the future when I was in the position he was in. As a guide.

I went home to a sleeping family and laid down for a bit. I oscillated between thoughts of "Screw this, I give up!" and "Just fix it." I finally fell asleep and woke the next morning to the second thought. I spent the next eight hours writing out those harms and was fully prepared for our next meeting later on that night.

When we got together for the next meeting we began and I had to start with something I had left out the night before. I wanted to hold some things back from him. There were many things I wished to take to the grave, things I swore I wouldn't tell another person in my life. Once this was done it was full speed ahead.

I weaved in those harms where they belonged in that timeline of my life and we retired for the second night after another five or six hours. As I left the flower shop I began to sense a lightness about me, about my thinking and about my heart. I was being set free from those bondages and that bondage of self.

On the third and final night we met again and it was absolutely frigid outside. A typical New England day as we approached winter. There were many revelations during the third night for me. All tied to the idea of having a shift from self-centeredness to

God-centeredness. For the first time in many years I began to think of others rather than myself and it began with thoughts of the mailman.

As I sat there spelling out all of my flaws and shortcomings, unraveling those defects of character for an examination with another man and God, it occurred to me what this guide was doing for me. The fact that he was giving of himself to this degree struck me hard. Especially when I looked across the table and saw that he was exhausted and had a pair of red laser beams for eyes. It occurred to me that he was spending time away from his own wife and home and was spending this night, and the past two, with another person trying to get him free from that bondage that can stick to so many of us like a wet t-shirt. His demonstration spoke to the last of the six principles the pioneers had learned were essential to keeping their God-consciousness. It was during this last night that I was given a glimpse of what my life would become in the near future when it came to being an agent for God. I would have to work with others in this same manner.

We finished our last night and I do believe he asked if there was anything that I left out in the writing. That "Is there anything you are trying to take to the grave or evade?" When I told him the barrel was now empty and clean he had one line for me before he gave me a hug and we finished with The Lord's Prayer.

"Welcome to Alcoholics Anonymous."

I had been attending those meetings for just over twenty-six years and this line struck me pretty hard. It showed me the deficiencies of what can be passed on to the newer attendees and even some of the older ones. In the time since that line was said to me it has brought with it new meaning as I set out to work with others and study the history of what these pioneers did, and found. Today I'm inclined to believe that it meant congratulations on finding what those pioneers found and enduring what they did to have their own spiritual experiences. That going to any length with a willingness to let go of all those old ideas. It was like a welcoming to a part of a society that can call themselves *recovered*.

As I approached that first day of this endeavor to confess my sins and even before I immersed myself in the writing there would be signs and it seemed as though there was this conspiracy on God's part to see me through it.

When I began this journey of the writing a gentleman reentered my life who was there when I first got sober, we belonged to the same group years and years before. This gentleman had gone through the process, and survived, only to be brought to a better life. A better vision of life. And God-consciousness. We spoke daily as I went through. He knew me and what position I was in. He knew how badly I was twisted. I remember placing a call to him and asking him to please come to the flower shop. He explained that he was busy and asked if he could come the following day. I explained that I needed him to come take my pistol and that I needed it gone, it was that bad. He showed up ten minutes later, walked through the front door, and put his hand out. I handed him the pistol. He turned and walked out without saying a word. I haven't seen the pistol since. He played another part in bringing me Home but that's for later in the story.

ROBERT ERNEST BACH

37 - A LEOPARD MAY NOT CHANGE ITS SPOTS BUT A MAN CAN

I came out of this experience feeling very light. Of course I had no clue what to expect in the way of how I was going to feel outside of the fact that my life would most certainly never be the same. I knew, and now another man knew, the depth of the depravity I'd been living. And I was at yet another turning point. I had another decision to make now.

I returned home that last evening again to a house where my family was sleeping. I sat alone for an hour and thought about the body of work that was just completed and recognized that I never had the power within myself to do it on my own and that there was certainly another Power at work here. Another Power that answered that petition to please come get me and bring me home and that this was the Path that was laid before me to take to get Home. I recognized that I had matched His favor with boatloads of willingness and a whole lot of raw and brutal honesty. There was just enough open space in that fissure to allow His grace to enter me provided my mind was open enough to try something different, after admitting my defeat in trying to right my own vessel. For me, this was nothing short of a miracle as I reflected on the twenty-three days of writing and the three night confession that just took place.

Before I passed out from exhaustion my thoughts ran to acknowledging the mailman's effort and time, and the sacrifice his own wife made by giving him the freedom to pass a gift on to me. A thank you card would be the least I could do and as this thought crossed my mind it was followed with a sort of amazement that yet again for the first time in many years I was thinking of someone else rather than myself, my own schemes and designs to try and play God.

I woke the next morning, the day before Thanksgiving, and started my contemplation. This lasted twenty-four hours, into the next morning. It became a wrestling match in the mind between that old self that was just fully revealed and a spirit within that was looking for a New Direction. The arguments went something like this.

"You weren't really that bad." Came the pleading whisper from Bad Bobby.

"Are you fucking kidding me? You're gonna listen to him after what you just endured?" Came the scream from that spirit within clamoring to be heard.

"You'll never, ever be able to clear the wreckage of your past, why bother?" The coaxing voice of the dying ego would say in a manipulative tone.

"There is more. So much more to this that I wish to show you, that I wish for you to experience, and to show others" Came the retort from the part of me that knew intuitively that anything is possible with effort. "After all it was just shown to you..."

This back and forth went on throughout the day as what would be a spiritual upheaval was slowly building from deep down inside. I didn't say much that day. I watched these thoughts go round and round as my wife carefully watched me throughout the day.

I passed out from mental exhaustion that night and would wake the following morning with a firm decision to keep trudging this Path that was set before me.

I woke up a bit more free with a resolve to keep moving forward, and into the next part of the process. That daunting action of seeking to right my wrongs. There were many to overcome.

My wife brought me a coffee and wished me a "Happy Thanksgiving." Up until this point I had followed the directions of a tour guide and it was now time to break from his guidance and begin to trust that inner voice within, my intuition which had been blocked by all those resentments, fears and harms, and follow the directions the pioneers had laid out, with the help of God. It was time to offer a different petition, prayer, to this Power, God. My contemplation was complete and I needed to keep going. There could be no rest now.

In their directions, mostly shared through their own personal experiences, they spoke to taking their book and placing it on a shelf and when ready taking it from that shelf and reciting a specific prayer. I asked my wife to please bring me my Big Book from downstairs and she did. When she returned to our bedroom I asked her to place it on top of the tall dresser.

"You just asked me to get the book for you!" As she tried handing it to me.

I refused to take it from her as if it were a hot potato and asked her again to place it on the tall dresser. With rolling eyes that said "I think he's losing his marbles" she placed it on the tall dresser. I'm not sure of the comment she made but I'm sure it was a good one to match the look in her eyes. She then left the bedroom and went back downstairs.

I was insistent on following the directions from this point; I didn't want to screw this up. I got out of bed and approached the tall dresser and took the book into my hand as if taking it down from a shelf. I even bent down a bit so that I was below it. Stop rolling *your* eyes! This was big for me to follow some form of direction, some rules, some sort of decorum, a set of laws or principles. I never had respect for any of that.

I opened this Big Book and read the prayer. I wouldn't understand the full meaning of the prayer for months after reciting it yet felt confident that it would work as it proved to do just that. I simply had to match God's favor with a continued willingness to work toward what was being asked of Him.

This was the third of three prayers said earnestly that would restore that covenant that I had broken with Him so many years before with that first resentment. It would require a tightening of that seatbelt for the ride I was about to continue.

This prayers reads as follows:

"My Creator, I am now willing that you should have all of me, good and bad. I pray that you now remove from me every single defect of character which stands in the way of my usefulness to you and my fellows. Grant me strength, as I go out from here, to do your bidding."[4]

I was indeed in that place of fully believing and knowing that God was my Creator when this prayer was offered, ironically on our day of thanks in America. I was expressing the fact that through the cataloging of my life and the awareness that I was without power for most it I was indeed ready to give myself completely to Him. That the "good and bad" encompassed every bit of it, and besides I had no clue what exactly was good or what exactly was bad, my intuition was still an infant and was going to need a workout in that gym of life. I tried my entire life to fix my mind, my heart, and to some extent even my soul and knew at this point that I not only failed to do this but that the power to achieve this end wouldn't be my own. I was not asking my New Parent to remove my shortcomings, my defects of character, my flaws, so that I might feel some relief. I was asking Him to do this so that I might be useful to *Him*. And for a man who was always trying to find an identity in life, a label, or even a way, or a front, or a new way to present my mask I was now Home. I had found an identity of real value, to not only me but to my wife and children, my family even if I'm estranged from them, to you the reader, and most of all to God. I was always hesitant to ask God for strength when I offered those "foxhole prayers" as I always believed

---

[4] See Bibliography

circumstances would be intentionally placed before me that would require an abundance of strength. I came to understand why strength was asked for at this point as I was just barely into the journey Home. The one question I simply needed to reaffirm was "Are you done living that way and ready to try something different?"

In many respects this prayer offered was an extension of that prayer said between the mailman and I. Almost like completing a sandwich, the first one was the first part, the bread, and the work in between, the meat. The meat being a test of willingness to be honest enough in seeking God. This last piece being the last piece of bread. The layer that would propel me into the next part of the work. The work of making amends.

I've had a most excellent experience in clearing that channel, with the undeniable help from God and the people he placed in my path along the way. It was this Power I came upon that redirected my ship and set me on a course to a real freedom. A freedom from self, ego, and pride. A freedom from feeling the need to play His part. What I once believed His grace to be, a rocky and tumultuous river current, has turned out to be the calmest sea. It's flat as a pancake and when ripples appear they are only on the surface and I can see them before they become tidal waves.

The greatest point the pioneers make in their offering is that once one becomes an alcoholic they have placed themselves in the position of being beyond human aid. There are many that believe they have the power within to change themselves and their own thinking. And their defects or shortcomings, whichever you prefer to label them. Many will exclaim "I'm working on that!" as a flaw is pointed out. I too once believed I could change myself but have come to know and understand that it is that One who has all of the Power that creates that change. I merely have to be willing when a flaw is recognized or seen, be honest enough to recognize its gravity, and have an open mind to let it go without covering it with claw marks.

ROBERT ERNEST BACH

38 - BEYOND HUMAN AID

The gentleman who came and retrieved my pistol from me during this process visited on more than one occasion. He was there through the entire journey and we now both stand on the same soil with a new set of roots firmly planted in God.

As I approached the writing with the mailman, Ronnie and I spoke daily and would discuss the journey, he sharing his own experience. He was there to witness it all. On the day I was to begin the confession the group that I still belonged to had a speaking engagement at a hospital before another group. Ronnie believed that it might be a good idea to skip this and to not speak before an audience. He was concerned that I would spill the content of my writing before a crowd. That would not have been pretty.

Yet I felt this *push* from within to go and speak. Speak to the fact that I had been attending those meetings for twenty-six years and was at last having a spiritual experience, share what I had been brought to. It would be a different "good news." I mentioned that when I knelt with the mailman it felt electric. Something was there. This was in fact at the beginning of that spiritual experience and from what I've learned from this it is exactly what I should be speaking to when sharing my experience with others. Ronnie's final suggestion to me was to go and make myself available to speak yet if I felt I couldn't do it eloquently and with some effect to simply stay seated and pass. He did not come to that meeting. He hasn't gone to meetings in years, yet lives in that God-consciousness.

I was able to speak with some effect and found that all I had to do was share what was happening and where I was in the journey. I spoke to where I landed at twenty-six years sober dry-firing a gun into my mouth and against the side of my head. To that feeling of wanting to check out. To all of those thoughts of madness in my mind. And then to the fact that I had just completed a twenty-three day endeavor in writing and would be starting my confession that very night. The mailman did come to the meeting that morning.

It was after this particular meeting that I was approached by three people who told me they were in that exact space of wanting to check out. These three people had just as much "time" as I and it moved me to tears that I was not alone in feeling this about the loss of something so essential to those beginning days of a great society, Alcoholics Anonymous. The *program* had been pushed aside in favor of the *fellowship*. At least in the area I live in, and I would come to find out that in many other areas as well as my life began to expand again. Finding out mostly through the internet and social media pages. The idea of the alcoholic, the spiritually sick, as being beyond human aid was brushed aside for the idea that somehow another human could somehow take the place of God. Much like right here and now in this space of time we are experiencing the same, as the word secular takes a greater place in our vocabulary than does the idea of God.

I came to understand what the pioneers called "rocketed into a fourth dimension of existence of which" I "had never dreamed."[5] My spiritual life expanded exponentially with the study of different principles and as dependencies on things human fell away. I left those meetings not because of a resentment or because I wasn't getting my own way. Those two reasons usually led to abandoning or dismissing things from my life in the past. I felt the last of those choking dependencies fall away as my trust and reliance on God became stronger and stronger. My God-consciousness was to be tested as I stepped closer to Him.

I often wondered why Ronnie walked away from the meetings yet lived comfortably. Not that comfortability of physical trappings, the comfortability with God and a renewed self free from that bondage.

As these dependencies on a group or different meetings were cut away there was a real sense of relief that washed over me. At first I was cautious, thinking it might be a trick of sorts that perhaps my mind or ego were playing on me to separate me from God. It was not a trick; it became a lesson in letting go

---

[5] See Bibliography

absolutely. A lesson in fully trusting and relying on God.

When I walked away from AA meetings my Facebook page and telephone blew up with messages. Not from those who wished for me to stay and not leave. They were from those who had done the same after having their own spiritual experience. Even the pioneers realized and stated that they knew very little of God, and perhaps little of what their lives would be like after these experiences. After all, they published their experiences after only a few short years after their own revolutionary changes in personalities.

While I do drop in to visit and look for a prospect to work with who might be craving a solution to their own problems, maybe that man who is holding that same pistol practicing his own exit from reality, I am no longer a member per se of the fellowship.

Those pioneers dropped a line in their Big Book that states that "Some of us tried to hang onto our old ideas and the result was nil until we let go absolutely."[6] Of course I offered that to you out of context yet the book is left open to interpretation. Most of those old ideas were the ones wrapped up in my own perception of God, and His will for me. Maybe a reference to those ideas that were a part of and had a hand in creating those guiding forces. Maybe the idea that I can play God. I've come to understand that it most definitely refers to those dependencies on things human, typically unhealthy.

---

[6] See Bibliography

Being, and living, free of dependencies became yet another demonstration of that Power for Him to use me, as He has used others, to show still others the possibilities that are there for all to enjoy.

ROBERT ERNEST BACH

39 - A LONG RECONSTRUCTION

The next few days in my journey seeking God by the path He set before me would be critical. My human nature, and that of many people I have met and worked with, not only alcoholics, have a tendency to take the easier, softer way while travelling through life. The most glaring example for me was when I left treatment and went to get my high school equivalency. I had the option of taking a few exams and collecting a real high school diploma but opted for taking quick five tests. I also believed I could take them all in one day. I always sought instant gratification.

The process of restitution, the action of seeking to right those wrongs I had done to others, those harms, might have provided one of those opportunities to again go for the effortless approach.

"They'll know you're sorry and remorseful when they see the change in you." That dying voice of the ego and pride whispered, looking to survive. But God countered with a voice that grew stronger in volume and seemed to have a bass attached to it that would thunder through a growing intuition. A sixth sense that I now had to come to rely on as God's voice within. A sixth sense that became refined and groomed through meeting with those I harmed.

On that Thanksgiving day I missed the first couple of courses of dinner as I was already on the telephone reaching out to my mother to arrange a time to meet so that I could come clean, if she was agreeable. The amends, the spoken part of it, happened during that call. The demonstration would take a few years to confirm the changes in me for her to fully believe that I was sincere.

I spoke to the amends made with my father and step mother way back in the writing; I've covered that one fully. Cataloging each one I was successful at and even the failures would hold us up. The point to be made here is that additional effort on my part was definitely needed and that the concept of righting all of the wrongs that I came across wasn't about me. It was not about setting *myself* free from my own past. It was about freeing all of the hostages I had taken throughout my life through my own spiritual malady and disconnect from God. It was about becoming an example of His Power and His Love. It was about a demonstration of living a different life grounded in a new set of principles. Principles I never had or could never adhere to as much as I would have liked to without His Grace. It was about losing an arrogance and gaining humility.

I learned even more about those guiding forces with each amends that I made. Ironically it was the most difficult ones, the amends I absolutely did not want to approach, that taught me the most. I believe I spoke to this when it came to my step mother.

Even when I attempted to make amends to my own sister I was rebuffed. We started speaking with one another as I was going through the writing and confession and knew she would be on that list of family members to make amends to. Our conversations began before I made amends to my father.

There is an underlying part of this principle of making restitution that necessitates no others be harmed in the process. I needed to have the conversation with my own sister to find out if my father knew that she knew what I had done in the past. I didn't want her to get dragged into my mess any further in the event she was brought up during the conversation. This led to more and more conversations with her. When I told her I would call her over the weekend and failed to do so and returned the call on the Monday instead she did not return the call. I saw her at the bank the following day and told her I called.

"You said you were going to call through the weekend. You didn't. You called on Monday. You'll never change." As she rolled up the window on her vehicle and abruptly ended the conversation. She was right. I didn't keep my word. Events led to another opportunity in the future yet all efforts to repair the damage that I did in this relationship did not work.

It was through the process of the amends that God began feeding me a new set of ideas, emotions, and attitudes that became the new *governor* of those guiding forces that needed to be set up. As I moved further into the repairing of my past it became crystal clear to me that I needed new guiding forces to live by.

There were indeed circumstances set in motion long before that fateful day that I combat-rolled out of my bed and begged God to take me home. Months before this I saw two of my family members split up leading to a divorce. Although my wife did scream those famous words "Get Out!" at me from time to time as my own mother and step mother had done I never listened to her. I didn't follow her direction. Though I knew if I didn't change eventually I would be served with divorce papers.

This impending divorce in my family rattled me to the core and was a bit of a harbinger for what might become of my own marriage. It became a tool in God's work of creating that fissure in my shell for His Light to enter.

My wife and I spent Thanksgiving Day at my uncle's ex-husband's apartment and the air about the scene was one of new beginnings. The new beginning for his now single life and my new beginning for my now God-conscious life. He was also well aware of what I had been doing through communication with my wife, and naturally supported this change.

He created this concoction of liquid and herbs that smelled medicinal and awfully pungent. He gave my wife instructions, he told her what to do with it later that night. It was a cleansing of sorts, ritualistic in nature. And after what I had just experienced it seemed appropriate. As appropriate as the period at the end of that last sentence and this one too. A marker of sorts to denote a definitive end and a new beginning.

I was to retire that night and take a hot shower cleansing the darkness away shifting the water to cold to lock it out. As I stood there dripping away in the symbolism of it all my wife was to pour this liquid over my head. I was not to rinse it off or towel myself dry. I was to wrap myself in a clean white sheet and go to bed while still damp with the concoction drying on me. We didn't have a white sheet so I wrapped myself in "Nana" and continued to bed. I cried and sobbed for an hour or so before I finally passed out.

I'm not sure if the tears, those big soupy splashy ones like those I had when I combat-rolled out of bed months before, shed that night were the result of the symbolism of his concoction, the result of that prayer I said that same Thanksgiving morning, the telephone call with my mother who readily accepted my verbal amends, or this.

My wife was still there. After all I had put her and our children through she was still there. There are times even today when I'll open my eyes in the morning and look at her and simply state with wonder, or question, in awe "You're still here?" My amends to my wife and children, although made verbally along the journey, began a couple of months before when I began taking the action in my life of solving my problems, with His Aid. The night she assisted me by dumping this cold liquid on me I knew she had already accepted my amends even if only to a small degree.

I woke up the following morning feeling a rest I hadn't felt in years, and there was this profound hope that I felt from deep within.

As far as I'm concerned today I'll be making

amends for the rest of my life at some level and a better part of them will come in the form of my demonstration of living in a different manner. With a simple attitude. Simple to verbalize and speak to but not so simple to express at times. Either expressed from the heart or on this physical plane. It is the attitude of trusting and relying on God in all things.

This brings me back to having my life rearranged with respect to my thinking and the physical. The physical I'll touch on later. But before I go there let me tell you that there were countless amends that had to be made on my part. And some of these will show up as we journey, through example, in what they taught me.

Though the amends will take a lifetime to complete the process of becoming God-conscious took just under four months for me and it was spent mostly in the midst of that spiritual upheaval where I walked around in pure bliss realizing I was free from that mind that wanted me dead.

I had to start somewhere to gain a bearing on a new set of principles that I could live by. A new set of ideas, emotions, and attitudes that could be built upon. The problem is that you can't walk into the local supermarket or deli and order them. They can't be bought. They're not sold at the mall or a farmer's market. As much as reading books in the past seeking answers had failed I would now have to do just that. I would have to take more action and do some studying.

I began with "The Four Agreements." A rudimentary and common sense way of living and a simple nourishment for a still infantile intuition that

DELUSION OF MIND STRENGTH THROUGH SPIRIT

was starving for sustenance. I spent seven days on each. I woke an hour earlier in the morning to read, studying the first one, and then spent an hour each evening doing the same before time spent in prayer and meditation. After seven days I moved onto the next one, and then the next, until I completed this month-long study. My wife dutifully woke me up for this in the morning with a cup of coffee and put the "Chill" station on the satellite radio for me. She quickly became a part of it. She participated in the process right along with me and I saw her buoyed by it. More on that one later in the writing.

I continued the study of different titles for months as I journeyed forward by God's Grace. I returned to a lot of the books I had read over the years and read them with a new set of lenses attached to my mind, and on my soul.

There is no doubt that I've done some pretty colorful things in my life and some of them landed in that area of my finances. This area would become the truest test of these principles I was trying to fit about me. The truest test of faith and the source of some of the worst fear I ever experienced.

I was shot into the spiritual upheaval with such force as though from a canon and placed squarely in the midst of a new life. Reborn. And there was absolutely, positively no way I could turn around and go back to living the way I had been, as a liar, a cheat or a thief. This meant potentially losing more and more of what I already had in the way of physical comforts. Whether it be a house or vehicle or anything else tangible in my life.

When I began this process just four short years

ago I was near 900,000$ in debt with a credit score somewhere in the 500's. It seemed an insurmountable amount to make amends for. Restitution. By trudging and trusting that I would not be dropped by God it has nearly all been resolved.

There were times when I would be gripped by a fear so debilitating that my mind wandered to checking out again but that option was quickly snuffed out like a flame. There were times while going through this that I heard the cock of that pistol I let go of so long ago and this was overdubbed with the assurance from God deep within my being that all I needed to do was trust Him. It *was* that mystery of faith.

In a short time my financial life was rearranged to match my new skin, my physical life came to resemble the tenor of my mind. It became sound. A commercial property I owned that had a compromised mortgage was easily dispensed of through negotiation and all I had to do was hand the keys to the investor. Through negotiation there was no adverse effect to my credit. With clear reasoning debts were paid and some of the bad debts simply fell away. The home that we were severely upside down on was sold short, also without having a bearing on my credit.

In my madness I mortgaged my mother's home to satisfy an expansion of my business and this fell into serious arrears. So much so that I was in danger of losing it which would have resulted in my mother not having a home. I tried with all of my might to restructure the loan and failed miserably. Placing the call to my mother in the midst of an already strained relationship with her to explain this was a blow to me.

It hurt like a son of a bitch yet would serve as one of those instances that bolstered the idea of trusting and relying on God.

When all hope was gone and I reached the end of all my options, which included a return to the mask that held the facade of thief, the miracle happened. My confidence was replaced with Godfidence. The day came when the bank reached out to me and explained that they were willing to modify the mortgage provided I live up to a new agreement. The mortgage is being paid, is now current, and the modification became a new agreement.

Where once my credit score was dismal it has drastically shifted to worthiness, a worthiness as strong as the worth of living a spiritual life based on a set of principles that are magical in their effect and an unwavering trust and reliance on my Maker that all will be well if I hold Him as my center.

ROBERT ERNEST BACH

40 - WATER SEEKS ITS OWN LEVEL

As I learned to use these new bearings and set to place them in motion I made some pretty wild observations. I went into my shed to retrieve something one day and counted seven gas cans. Apparently every time I needed gas the thought crossed my insane mind that maybe I needed a gas can too. Obviously I followed this thought a few times while under the malaise of that spiritual malady.

As I tried to fit myself to be of maximum service to God and other people I counted six surround sound systems about the house and in the basement. Apparently there was something so attractive about shiny and new stuff that I couldn't resist while suffering from that disconnect. I counted five satellite radio receivers too. I couldn't stay away from spend therapy: that spending money I didn't have to make myself feel better.

As a friend visited the flower shop one day with his teenage daughters and one of them wanted to know the password to my laptop to show me something online I turned to her and said "Fuck You." Everyone just looked at me like I was an asshole and looked like they wanted to run. I quickly had tell them that this was the password. Today my password is "Trust God."

There must have been something about trash cans that had an allure that couldn't be resisted. Maybe I thought I could stuff some of that over spilling pain from my own barrel into them because I had ten of those.

As I came to realize how much I had I also came to realize how very little I really needed in this life when it came to physical things. I had grown accustomed to driving a Land Rover over the years and this became important to me as a part of my persona, my mask, and what I cared for you to see and how I wished to be seen. As I shifted away from a stance grounded in ego to one of humility this would fall away too. In Rhode Island there is this thing about having a four-digit numbered license plate, a *vanity* plate, and I was ecstatic when the dealership managed to get me one. One of the best moments of my life, a closing of that door on the potential possibility of returning to my old life, was when I walked into the Division of Motor Vehicles and turned that plate in. Even the lady behind the counter looked at me like "Really? You want to let go of this?" I recall thinking to myself with a chuckle as I walked away "You have no idea what I've just let go of in my life!"

As the answer to that age old question of why we are here wrapped in these meatsuits shifted from a short and shallow response to an answer that was now being appreciated and explored at deeper and deeper levels, gaining serious weight, my life continued to become more and more valuable to me. And I hope to God and His divine purpose. I'm confident it has as I now can feel this without the hazy shadows of resentments and fears, guilt and shame for harms I caused, and with the look of the men I work with today.

My sound reasoning has been restored as a result of the work I did and continue to do today. My physical life changed from within and also the without. Not only would I experience a change in my physical appearance by losing those black circles around my eyes from lack of sleep or too much of it I am now without any medications whatsoever. High blood pressure is gone. Cholesterol levels are normal. And that anxiety and depression and even that ADHD? Gone.

The without changed slowly to match the tenor of my spirit as well as a result of seeking God and addressing all of those things that blocked me from Him. I was driving home one evening and felt as though everyone was flying by me on both sides. When I looked down at the speedometer I was actually going near the speed limit. This is just one small example of how a shift happened within to effect every area, on the outside, of my life.

Where I once felt a hopelessness in my business and was growing weary of it my wife and I were able to recreate it. We moved it to a different market where what we offered in design matched the area. Our client base came to match our *new* ideas, emotions, and attitudes.

It became clear to me that the adage of water seeking its own level applies to our personal lives as well. Chances are if I'm living an ungodly life as a liar, a cheat, and a thief I'm surrounded by the same. And conversely, if I'm living a God-centered life trying to live by the four absolutes, absolute honesty, absolute unselfishness, absolute love, absolute purity, placing God above and before all else, my life will be surrounded by the same.

These are extremely tall orders to live by in our jungle of a world and can be as equally difficult to practice in mind and thought. And through extension, seeing these qualities in all things, and people, can be difficult. It requires that virtue of patience, a spirit of love for all, a kindliness to be extended no matter the grounds, and a tolerance that is easy to come by after you recover from that spiritual malady.

PART SIX

WE'RE NOT JUST HUMAN

41 - GO FORTH AND DEMONSTRATE

As we make a turn into the final leg of my writing, and sharing, of what has been and is my life I wish to thank you with all that I have within me for being here. My spirit within salutes the spirit within you. Your authentic self. If you are still with me on this journey then perhaps something has resonated with you and for this I am deeply touched. As deeply touched as I was by that mailman with his efforts and by the many men and women that I have had the opportunity to work with as they journeyed home to God.

As I floated in that bliss of a spiritual upheaval and continued to make amends I quickly learned more about what those pioneers had discovered. The first thing evident to me was that as this relationship with God was restored, recovered, I needed to increase my time spent with Him. It was like any relationship that we have, it is built on spending quality time getting to know one another. The best way for me to do this was and is through prayers that I offer, thoughts that seem to be transmitted through that freshly-cleaned channel. Time spent in meditation getting to know this new vital sixth sense and how to listen to it. It being the house that held those answers to my prayers.

I also had to do some heavy duty exercises when it came to easing back into the flow of life. My work, relationships, society and to a great extent my thoughts. This was not easy for me. There were many nights and waking moments when I would stand in the middle of that garden of good and evil in bewilderment, lost for answers. There were many moments of indecision, moments of confusion, and moments of despair.

Indecision because I was afraid to decide upon anything for fear of making a mistake and causing someone pain. Moments of confusion because those new ideas, emotions, and attitudes were so weakly formed and despair because I felt like a child. And in many respects I was still a child, learning.

There were many who "just showed up" out of the blue and became a part of my life as tall strong trees planted firmly in God's soil while my roots were nourished through learning how *to be*.

Even though those old ideas, emotions, and attitudes were cast aside and I could no longer live by them my mind hadn't fully recovered from the allure of them. There were so many instances where my mind wanted to resort to its old way yet there was this new resistance to acting out on those thoughts. It seemed as though what the therapist had told me was indeed correct. Where I once went from thought to heart without a pause there in truth was one after my thoughts now. I was able to just *see* them. The problem I had was with 60,000 thoughts a day, I grew extremely tired and irritable. It was moments such as this that I had that simple choice. Either turn to God or succumb to the madness.

I waded back into the flow of life like someone trying to get used to cold water in a pool. Slowly and one toe at a time. As I did this I commenced to study that Big Book on a daily basis and each time I did I gained in appreciation for what those pioneers had found and now, more importantly, how their reactions to life were drastically changed. What they did to begin living a spiritual life versus an ungodly life.

They spoke to the fact that even though I had a spiritual awakening there would still be times when I would get hit with a resentment or a fear, selfishness would show up and even dishonesty. They shared that what they had found was that the spiritual life had to be *lived*, that it is real and not just a theory, an ideal. Even the good doctor who offered his own opinion about what he witnessed in those who recovered spoke to the fact that an alcoholic who has placed himself beyond human aid could never survive on some bubbly, he used the word "frothy," application. He intimated that one would need something with "depth and weight." My relationship with God provides this for me as does an effort to reach others.

There are still occasions when a resentment will pop up out of the blue and each comes with their own book of lessons to be learned. Maybe the answer to the question as to why some humans can shrug off a resentment easily and let it go and some cannot may never be answered. Most times I am successful in just *watching* them, as if detached, yet at other times they come out of that calm sea that is stretched all around me like Jaws. And they're indeed seeking to destroy me, or more to the point, my God-consciousness, my relationship with God. It's like they are looking for safe harbor in that channel where they know they have their own power to squelch that Light if allowed.

The fears that do arise on occasion seek to do the same yet for some reason I have the ability to see them with a clarity, a clarity to know to turn to God almost immediately. They don't seem to get their teeth into my mind, or peace.

Each seem to carry a darkness with them.

As I continue my journey home to God and make myself available to be of use to Him by recognizing that He is the parent and I the child, that He is the Director and Principal and I simply one of His agents I become more enlightened to what exactly He wishes for me to be. And that is tied to my intuition. When I began this journey I was simply one of his many, many soldiers without any kind of ranking.

As I continued to recover and get stronger, as I came to believe in His Power, and as I worked out my intuition like it was a muscle being worked out in a gym, as I explored this mystery of my new faith I became aware that there were forces all about me. Some were brilliant and bright enough to make me squint and others just downright dark and nasty. I recognized the dark ones easily as I had experienced that kind of existence for years. The bright ones became easier to recognize as I continued. They were inspirational, the bright lights, the souls connected by an unwavering faith.

I've found that as I journeyed farther away from the darkness and closer to the Light there would, at times, be forces from the past, forces from others with that darkness, a force that would love nothing more for me to succumb to it and walk away from God. My friend, I'll call him Rock, termed it perfectly one night when I was feeling somewhat battered by someone filled with that darkness. He expressed that the darkness has just as many soldiers without rank as does God. And that the darkness can knock off any of God's soldiers with very little effort but its real prize is pulling down one of God's officers. His agents that try to keep their eyes set upon Him, one who tries to be dutiful for Him.

I'm not trying to speak to you from some lofty mountaintop or in a condescending manner by using this analogy. I'm not that powerful and that's not the conclusion I'm trying to impress on anyone. What I'm trying to express, maybe clumsily, is that there is a difference in my life today. I do not believe I'm any closer to God than anyone else nor do I practice prayer or meditation better or worse than anyone. I do know that as I continue to seek Him, thereby getting closer to Him, I can clearly see and feel His favor. And as this is happening I am called to do things I never imagined in this life and they're not always easy yet when I know deep within what God has done for me, things I tried to do and never succeeded at, I don't hesitate. I just follow that gut feeling in the solar plexus. I embrace my promotion in rank.

The pioneers left us their experience and with it many predictions as a result of their own spiritual awakenings, and one bold promise. When a recovered alcoholic made that approach to another alcoholic, one of the founders of AA, to offer him a solution to his problems the one that was approached asked him how he did it. How he got sober. His response was as selfless and as complimentary as could be to his own Maker. He gave God the credit and simply told the alcoholic that God had done it for him.

This is what has happened to me.

I never had the power.

God did.

And all that was necessary was a willingness to meet Him. To get and be honest with Him. And to be open to seeking Him further.

42 - ADVANTAGES FOR ALL

As I continued to explore this relationship with God there were so many highs and lows. As I exercised my new thoughts that sprung forth from those strengthening guiding forces I made mistakes. Perfection is a great ideal when it comes to living a spiritual life and one I try to hold dominant in my mind yet it is only that, an ideal, it is not always reality. Only the progress toward this ideal is possible unless I somehow find a way to ascend the Earth.

When I came out of the spiritual upheaval that shifted my personality I swung like a pendulum between the absurd and downright loftiness in thought and action to a reality grounded in common sense. I continued reading books and studying. I continued to wade into the flow of life exercising my mind and intuition. I continued to see that the trappings of life, the house, the cars, the clothes, the stuff, were really not that important when reduced to their right place as I was being right-sized.

As I was exploring I thought that maybe I had to travel to some foreign country to learn how to meditate properly. I thought that I should go live in a hut and live off of the land. In other words it took quite some time for the dust from the storms within my mind to settle down and fade away.

The personality change that I experienced was abrupt and became part of my demonstration but when I first came out of it I was your typical overzealous "you have to have what I found" nut. Thankfully this tempest calmed as well.

After spending twenty-six years trying to apply a set of twelve principles to my life without an understanding as to how it was to be done with the most effect and finally having such a great experience the thought occurred to me that in that time I had failed so many that I had worked with. As my mind turned to them I would reach out and simply share what I had found, what God had brought me to, and my experience. This began the working with others that would deepen not only my appreciation for my own experience but my understanding of what those pioneers had found. And as I went deeper into this work I was to see that my experience matched the words they had written decades before more and more.

At the very beginning of their writing they express that this way of life, this design for living, not only has advantages for the alcoholic, but for all. This is exactly what I have witnessed in my own journey.

Life with an alcoholic who is drinking is no doubt a tiresome one. A life with an alcoholic who has failed to have a spiritual experience and yet is without the alcohol can be as equally tiresome, taxing. Both are damaging. The effects are downright nasty and brutal upon the spirit of any that are close to the alcoholic who has yet to recover a connection to

God. The pioneers stated that many don't realize just how sick the alcoholic is, and most times a sober alcoholic won't realize how sick they are until they find themselves in the position I was in at twenty-six years sober. Unfortunately, those who love the alcoholic, the spouses and family and even friends become infected as well and don't even know it. Alcoholism has to be one of the most misunderstood, and downright insidious, illnesses of all time. The spiritual malady is real yet easily denied by the sufferer and those about the sufferer. Nearly every person has been touched by it.

As much as my recovery from this illness has benefited me and reconnected me to God, the practice of my God-consciousness and exploration of it has certainly changed my life physically. Part of that physical aspect extends to those around me. My wife, my children, my family, my friends, my associates and clients.

My son no longer walks around the house asking his mother "Why don't you divorce that fucking asshole?" My wife no longer has to wonder what my reactions will be and can almost predict a strong level of acceptance on my part for whatever comes with the flow of life. There is more but the point I was reaching for and trying to make is this.

As much as there was a disgust on my family's part with me at some level there lurks this denial as well. A denial that something needs to change, insidious huh? At some level as much as one who loves an alcoholic wishes for that same person to get better and to change for the better, when this does happen the one who wished for it doesn't like it or want it to be better. That is the infectiousness of spiritual sickness. It gets under the skin of those around the sufferer and they grow ill as well.

As I came out of that state of bliss it occurred to me that my life would never be the same and that there were certainly going to be some drastic changes spiritually, and both mentally and physically. And there were going to be choices made not only on my part but on the part of my wife. To some extent I infected her and she had to decide whether to take this journey with me or refuse. Thankfully she and I have journeyed this recovery of sanity and God-consciousness together. It was not easy yet it was simple when we centered our lives in God and made God the center of our lives.

I have learned not to apologize for my belief in God and have found that it is courageous to have a faith and further courageous to exercise that faith with a clear demonstration. For years I would hide the fact that I was on my knees when praying. I would kneel before the toilet and pray much like I knelt before the toilet when puking drunk. I kneel regularly and have no desire to hide this action anymore.

As much as I tried different meditations and thought to seek different lands to learn how to meditate properly it was through two gentlemen on the internet that turned me onto a meditation that reminds me of what those pioneers had found. That my Creator is within my heart, and is a part of me, as a feeling is deep down within me, directly tied to my intuition. And that I am as much a part of Him as He of me.

This is the state I live in at most times and the only thing that can shift me from this position are those moments of weakness when I am taken for a ride by a resentment, or a fear born out of a resentment.

As I came out of this process and began my own search for God I was faced with this mountain of debt that seemed impossible to clear away, amend. I don't have to share the specifics as there is a pretty good chance you have had financial difficulty and that will suffice and give you an idea of the fear I felt. What happened was this.

As my fear surfaced and then some resentment toward self appeared for good measure I attempted to do exactly what I tried to do my entire life. I fell off of the Path and attempted to put the God-shirt back on. I grew impatient with my new Director and thought that He should be working faster to resolve all of it. (It doesn't work like that.) I grew to be uneasy, annoyed, and dissatisfied as if I had never changed. The thought to off myself returned and I became scared. I didn't know what to do and when I spoke with others who had been through the process of recovery in my local area I was unable to find one who had this same experience. None could make a suggestion for a remedy based on experience.

I reached out to two men who were on a social media page who I admired for their own understanding of this design for living and asked for their assistance. Both had spoken to a meditation they did and that became a part of their own seeking of God. One of the men digressed from the conversation and left it to the other to keep going with me. In just two days I was back on the path and handed God His shirt back with an apology. The meditation saved me from fully faltering back into a state of unconsciousness and brought about a deeper understanding of what it was I was really saying or asking for in prayer.

The eleventh step of the Alcoholics Anonymous program reads as follows...

"Sought through prayer and meditation to improve our conscious contact with God *as we understood Him,* praying only for the knowledge of His will for us and the power to carry that out."[7]

The implication with this step and the writing of it is that the word "we" be placed before it as it was the pioneers collective experience, and its written in the past tense as are all of the others.

I understood the intent of this for years, the improving of my contact with God yet always stumbled when it came to that one profound word dropped in the midst of this ideal. That word is *"only."*

When I was shot out of that cannon and became aware that there was indeed a God and that he wasn't out to get me or drill me into the ground and as I began to learn how to pray I would naturally beg for relief from a great many things. I would, while in the midst of the fear that surrounded the reparation of relationships, ask for specific things like a petulant child on Santa Clause's lap. I asked for relief from the financial burdens and the troubles they were causing, again asking with specificity. The prayers I offered were still wrapped in that garment of selfishness and self-centeredness.

The act of meditating not only revealed where

---

[7] See Bibliography

exactly God could be found but also led me to understand that by asking for specific things with an air of selfishness I was indeed playing God. I was trying to tell Him what to do. Trying to sway Him. I've come to know and understand that He indeed knows exactly what I am in need of before I even state it. I've come to understand that His plan is as definite for me as is His exact design for everything in nature, those flowers, those trees, even the ugly ones, the oceans and the life within, the animals in all of their kingdoms and so on and so on and so on.

All I need do is make myself available to be of service to Him and listen for His directions. Sometimes when He speaks it is a simple whisper like a soft breeze and I have to listen hard. Other times he yells loudly with a lot of that bass that rocks my intuition causing me to carry on the battle as not just a soldier in His army but as an officer. This is of course an honor to be trusted with as I work with others.

(You may find the links for the meditation I referenced at the end of the Epilogue.)

ROBERT ERNEST BACH

43 - THE POWER OF A DEMONSTRATION

As I came out of the writing and the confession and it became apparent that I would no longer be living by a loose set of principles, bouncing through life in my meatsuit like that pinball in the big machine, seeking to only pleasure my need to be satisfied, there was a long period of reconstruction. This repairing was not limited to my mind, heart and soul or limited to my physical life. I had to demonstrate a new set of ideas, emotions, and attitudes and in the beginning it was certainly clumsy. It was similar to a baby learning to walk or speak, the confusion at times was equally as awkward as I imagine it is for that baby.

The main point I wish to make here is that when drastic changes are experienced from within and one is set on a new course it is noticed. At times it is noticed by those outside of the one who experienced those changes long before it is in the one who has had the transformation. A clear example is how those who surround the alcoholic who is drinking recognize the problem and attendant chaos long before the drinker sees it, if they are even fortunate enough to wake from the madness. The same holds true when an alcoholic experiences a drastic personality change through the twelve steps. It is seen by those who surround the changed person in a pronounced way. It is clearly evident that Something is at work in this person.

I had loose morals and values while my spirit was disconnected from God and under the spell and madness of the ego, that lower self. At times they were non-existent, there was absolutely no pull from what little conscience I had in me, sober. There was a time as I lumbered my way through life without consciousness that any behavior was acceptable to me. In my early recovery there were very few young people in recovery and those of us who were did get together. One of our circle was not of legal age, I was. As we grew closer in our own madness's she and I fell into bed together. Although we were two consenting people a line was crossed, by me. Although it was short-lived it had a bearing on each of us, a bearing that would stretch a couple of decades. The bottom line is that this was a situation where I harmed another spirit. Even though the consent was there it was wrong and went against the grain of any sharpened morals and values. Both a moral and legal law were broken. When the gravity of what I had done collided with that bit of consciousness I distanced myself from her.

As time went on and my life expanded I married. After a short period this marriage became filled with madness and became fraught with division as did many relationships in my life. I separated from my wife for a few weeks and went to stay with a friend, a friend who was another in that circle of young people in recovery. This young lady was now an adult and lived in the apartment above my friend. Each time I looked into her eyes I felt that pull of guilt, shame and remorse for what I had done.

As I left for work one morning I called upstairs to see if she needed a ride to work and she accepted. As we drove I handed her a matter of fact verbal apology for what happened. It became a silent ride in the car. After I returned home to my wife I didn't see her for quite a few years and when we were reconnected it was through social media.

The verbal apology I offered her while driving was insufficient. It was not enough. There was no demonstration to back it up as my consciousness remained dark and dull for years after this. Each time I saw her image on social media and her posts I felt this pull within, a longing to right a wrong. This longing wasn't a need to set myself free, it was a desire to release her from whatever she might be carrying from that interaction; her own ideas, emotions, and attitudes and resultant guiding forces.

As I began to get used to the new skin that was replacing the one shed through the process of the twelve steps and consciousness began to dwarf my old way of life I was forced to go out to those I had harmed. I made direct arrangements to do this with many people and many were by happenstance. The amends to this spirit came about by the latter.

I was about eight or nine months into the process and was lounging on a Sunday afternoon by the pool with my wife, each of us with our faces buried in our smartphones or the books we were reading. My device chimed and as I looked at the screen it was a message from this young lady that was indeed on that list of many I had to make amends to. As we began shooting messages back and forth I intuitively knew that this was one of those instances where God creates the circumstances in our favor to either step up or step away. I knew He was handing me an opportunity to right a wrong. As we went deeper into conversation I simply asked if we could get together and speak. She replied that she knew exactly what I wished to do and there was no need to do so, that she had let it go years before. It felt as though I was getting off a little too easy yet as the conversation progressed it became clear that she had indeed made peace with that time in our lives.

She explained that in the time we were connected on social media she had been watching me. She had been watching my transformation from afar. This is how powerful our demonstration of a new set of principles, a new design for living, can be. It is noticed, even on social media. The demonstration of what happened to me, the easily-visible changes seen through the tenor of my behavior and postings on a Facebook page, created her own place of arriving at forgiveness. A release from an interaction that undoubtedly added to her own guiding forces. Her passing of forgiveness to me was shown to me by the messages sent following this.

She explained that she had indeed witnessed what happened with me. (It served as a great validation as there were many times when I wished to throw in the towel.) She explained that she was having difficulty with her ex, the father of her son, and his family and that there might be a period of time when her son would be removed from her. She explained that it might be a period of six months and that I was the only person she could trust to take him for her. She wanted him to be safe. This was pretty explosive and as I read this I was floored on many different levels.

I told you that I was lounging next to my wife. My wife was trying to get used to my new skin as well and her trust in my new position in life was still far from being solid at this point. She had no knowledge of this part of my past, few did. I pointed out the levels of this interaction that were touched and this would bring nuances of many flavors. And awakenings.

The "old me" would have immediately responded with a decision based in selfishness, without consulting my wife and children about the idea of helping another. I would have opened the door to my home that day yet my response was to simply relay that I had to discuss it with my wife. The "new me," governed by sound reasoning, was now stronger than the old me, peculiar thought driven by selfishness, ego. This young lady understood and I messaged that I would reach out later on in the day.

This brought me to an unfamiliar place, a place that was still being worked out in the gym, the place of having to walk through fear or brush it aside, evasion. It would have been simple to respond a few hours later and state that it wouldn't work, lie. It would be more difficult to have the conversation with my wife about a period of time in my past leading up to the present ending with handing her this request from another who was a stranger to her, truth.

As a consequence of this young lady being freed from our interaction so many years ago I was also freed from it. That's always the upside to cleaning up our pasts. This freedom fueled the courage to come clean with my wife and make this request. Yes, it was an uncomfortable conversation to have yet when God calls you out of the dugout to be of service to Him the call must be answered no matter the cost, especially to the destruction of selfishness and self-centeredness. Yes, the conversation did come with questions posed to me by my wife, questions that would clear up her doubts about my new skin at an even deeper level. As my wife and I ended the conversation it was agreed that we would indeed make ourselves available and would answer that call that came out of the Dugout.

In the end this young lady did not have to take these actions and everything worked out perfectly for her and her son. As I approached this manuscript and knew this interaction might land on the pages I reached out to this young lady to gain her consent for its inclusion. Happily for you, her, and I, she agreed. Each time I see her posts on social media I'm reminded of the awesome power held within these principles that can brought about with a willingness to trudge them.

44 - INTERMEZZO NUMBER TEN

As I learned to come to terms with my humanness while recognizing and recovering that spirit within that I was shot onto the planet with, a spirit readily installed deep within that was fortunate enough to survive the battering of all those flippers in the pinball machine, my eyes were opened wider and wider to humanity around me. I started to see the failings of not only my own will but those around me and could see spiritual disease in others clearly. It can be disconcerting and mind-boggling. Especially when I looked at everything else that seemed to follow the laws of nature without hesitation, or resistance. It was this awakening that would inspire my effort to start that chore I felt that I was set here for. The chore of trying to reach others as I had been reached and this is where I was schooled in the difference between that sometimes, more often than not, injurious self-will and empowering God's will.

I came to that sixth principle of those original six, continued work with other alcoholics, while trying to adhere to or live by those four absolutes. As I went about this work it became clear to me, and rather quickly, that most really don't want to solve their problem while under the auspices that there isn't an issue to begin with outside of their drinking. On the flip side of not walking away from the work, there were gains in understanding of just how raw spiritual sickness can be. Whatever was not uncovered through my own moral inventory or confession and even those amends was revealed through the effort of trying to reach others. And undoubtedly through their failures, as well as mine in the past. Those pioneers recognized that when self-examination, prayer, and meditation failed to keep them on the path, from slipping back into unconsciousness, working with another would save the day.

I've witnessed many men and women reach the writing of the moral inventory, and then fall off of it. And those who made it through the confession trudge on only to fail at the action of the amends. They lost the steam to keep going and fell off too. And I've witnessed still less who have made it through the amends process fail to keep up the work of remaining God-consciousness by remaining vigilant while watching and just observing along with prayer and meditation. And still even fewer make it to the point of serving God as one of His agents. They either went back to sleep or drank. And of those who did fall or drank and made it back to the path the numbers were relatively low. It was the observation of this that inspired to me to keep moving forward. The option of going back to sleep was taken off of the table. Much like I wanted to be that one in twenty that made it after treatment I wanted to make it in this area too. And besides, once I received a taste of God's mercy, and then His Glory, I couldn't go back into that barrel and recreate the crap I lived while in that darkness.

The pioneers found that they were most effective while working with others after they themselves had gone through the process. They came upon their God and a full appreciation of what the real problem was, the spiritual malady, not just a drink problem, the symptom and extension of the illness. And being placed in this position they were empowered to be of better use to their God and others. They had received a promotion in rank in His army. And with this promotion came an awesome responsibility, to their God and to others who might be willing to do the heavy lifting.

The most absolute cruelest thing you can tell an alcoholic is "Don't drink." A real alcoholic does not enjoy this luxury other men or women who do not have that body allergy or mental obsession have. If they had a choice of not drinking there would most likely be no problem, and those two words wouldn't be said out loud. Yet this is at most times what happens when a potential or real alcoholic is told while in a treatment facility or even when they have the courage to crawl into an AA meeting. "Don't drink and go to meetings."

But the man or woman who has had a spiritual awakening as a result of doing that heavy lifting can be the difference between life and death not only for the alcoholic and his family but the innocent bystander who might have the misfortune of being in their way.

Try this parable on for size.

It's a Monday morning after another one of "those weekends." The weekend that ends with silence as the Missus finally falls asleep after watching her husband drink throughout it. Intermittently screaming and yelling at her and his children. He makes it to work with a resolve to stay sober, not drink. And is successful, this day. He even manages to get home without pulling into that beacon that is shining bright along the way, the liquor store. The one where the bottles speak to him of the false promise of solving his problems. They are together as a family at the dinner table and manage to get through dinner although you can cut the silence, and tension, with a knife.

The next morning, with the same resolve about him, he manages to get to work and gives his wife and children a kiss goodbye with the promise to return for dinner later that day. He muscles his way through the day with some nervousness about him and thinks it best to take a different route home as that beacon of light now seems to have added a loud whistle to it. He makes it home to dinner and because he hasn't had a drink in two days there is a sense of hope when he arrives there. The look in his wife's eyes speaks to it. She believes that he has finally licked his problem. The children even venture a joke or two and even risk sharing about their own day at school looking for some kind of recognition or approval from their Dad. He manages to get back into the big bed that night although his advances are rebuffed by his wife. He passes out from the mental exhaustion of trying to stay sober all day with a bit of his own false hope about getting lucky the next night.

On Wednesday he rises to coffee and their seems to be a spirit of forgiveness about the kitchen as everyone is gathered at the breakfast table. His spirits are high as he leaves the house and begins to fall further into the delusion that he is exercising some kind of control over his mind, and drinking, on his own power. He's not as shaky this day and the smell of alcohol that some around him can swear they are smelling beneath that strong cologne and breath mints has left him now. He feels clean and his sense of accomplishment strokes his ego and pride. He manages to gather in the family room that evening and watch a Disney movie with the kids before they are tucked in and later in the evening manages to have his advances accepted by his wife. After all, the dust from his last storm in temper and words has sort of settled without the drink in him.

The next day his confidence is stroked by his ego and some compliments on his performance and attentiveness at his job. The boss seems pleased and he manages to elicit a few smiles and "atta boys" from his co-workers. Yet he is exhausted from what seems to be a battle in his own mind, a battle painfully brushed aside and shielded by delusion. He feels powerful and this fuels the delusion. "I've got this. I can do this!" He returns home that evening and finds that there is a sitter there for the kids, and his wife has planned a night out for them, a dinner in a cozy restaurant. He hasn't been around alcohol since the weekend yet feels confident. During dinner he misses the plans his wife is speaking of for the upcoming weekend for them and the kids. All he can see are the drinks all over the place and each is speaking to him. Enticing him to please come back. "You're weren't that bad, you controlled it all week. See, you can control it. You made too much of it, she made too much of it." Words he would hear all day while at work Friday. Payday.

He wakes up a bit shaken but still exuding confidence. "I've got this." He muscles his way through the day, uncomfortably. The voices he heard from all of those drinks the night before begin speaking to him. And they grow louder in their appeal and stronger in their romantic persuasiveness. He hasn't had a drink yet in his mind he is already there. The mental obsession has already pushed aside whatever frail and fragile resolve and sound reasoning he appeared to be exercising all week long. He typically brings his paycheck home for his wife, for the mortgage, for the groceries and needs of his family but tonight he won't.

He leaves work and turns his cell phone off. He doesn't stop at the liquor store to satisfy that mental obsession, he heads straight to the pub where he knows the bartender will be glad to cash his check. As he enters he feels a shift. A sense of relief pours over his mind and his spirit. He's home. And thinks that he'll be able to have just one or two drinks. But in what seems to be a blink of an eye he is already well past the number of drinks he really thought he could limit himself to. Once the alcohol enters his body that thought is easily tossed aside in favor of keeping the party going. He is now under the baffling spell of that phenomenon of craving and can't stop as much as he wants to, even as those images of his wife and children and thoughts about their plans for the weekend try to enter his mind. It is too late. He is off and running.

At his already delicate home his wife is left to wonder. And assure the kids that everything is "fine." And with that come the excuses she is so used to handing to them. As the night comes to an end and the kids are finally asleep she sits in the living room. Waiting. And hoping. Waiting and hoping for her husband, who seemed to have the problem licked, to walk through the door. With a plausible reason for his lateness. Thoughts that maybe he is hurt fueled by her own false hope and delusion shift to a resignation that he is drinking and she cries herself to sleep.

When the wife and children wake the next morning and his car isn't in the driveway the sour atmosphere that was in the home the weekend before returns with a scent that is stronger. He has never been gone overnight before. His wife walks around the house in a daze all day and into the night as he never comes home that Saturday. As much as the young children try to occupy themselves and "stay out of the way" they are more occupied with their father's absence and the week old memory of the previous weekend. All three of them fall into a despair that they are as powerless over this as the husband and father is over that mental obsession. As much as the mother wishes to lie to her children she finally confides, admits, what the problem is and the three of them begin seeking God in prayer, together. Three as one. They all sleep in the same bed that evening and the wife cries herself to sleep as the children sleep lightly and restlessly.

The husband and father will not recall this day. He is now in a blackout.

On the Sunday the husband and father comes to, late in the afternoon. He is dirty, covered in grime and scents he picked up that weekend from his promiscuity. His money is gone. He spent every bit of his paycheck. After he manages to locate his vehicle he returns home and walks in the door as if all that has happened is normal, a very natural part of life, yet he is also baffled at this turn of events. The children are ecstatic that he is home and instantly feel the hope that everything is going to be okay. His wife does not show this same joy, or hope. Her delusions are smashed and she is at the end of her rope.

The children go to sleep and do so more comfortably than the night before. As the evening wears on and he is hammered by his wife with threats and accusations he is worn down and agrees that he is powerless and needs help with his problem, that symptom alcohol, that accompanies spiritual illness. He refuses treatment at a facility or a hospital and agrees he needs to go to "one of those AA meetings." He agrees to find out where one is the next day while at work and will go the very next evening. His wife feels more hope than she had felt in years.

The next day he does much the same as he had the previous Monday. He muscles through the day and manages to stay away from a drink. He also manages to find out where a meeting is that night. He returns home after work and has dinner which is eerily the same as the week before. There aren't many words spoken and then he leaves the house. Although his wife is hopeful he will make it to the meeting and then return home she has her doubts. Her and the children say another prayer when he leaves the house.

This husband and father, a real alcoholic, manages to ignore that lighted beacon screaming at him as he passes the liquor store on the way to the meeting. He walks into this strange place and is welcomed by outstretched hands and manages to start a conversation with another fellow there before the meeting begins. He gets a cup of coffee and sits down, listens to the speakers each telling their tale. Most of them speak about their drinking, something he already knows plenty about. He hears war stories of debauchery and not much else as this is what is spoken to during the meeting. At the end of the meeting he's not feeling much better.

He already knows how to drink, he has that part down perfectly. He mustered whatever power he had left in him to get there dripping with desperation for a solution to the madness in his life, and in his mind. At the end of the meeting he speaks to that same fellow and asks him how to stay sober.

"Don't drink and go to meetings." is what this man tells him.

One of the saddest parts of this story is that this is what happens each and every day to men and women looking for a solution. Most times it's not there and many simply languish and will shuffle from meeting to meeting and will have to settle for a lower level of comfort than what those pioneers were able to offer after they had experienced their own awakenings of spirit. The next part that is equally as sad is that all of those things that happened to this man over a week's time can still take place in a man or woman even after they put the drink down and remain sober if they do not have the fortune of experiencing a change of personality, a spiritual awakening. A spiritual experience that sets them on a course to recreate their own lives.

The man or woman who has recovered that relationship with their Maker and is well aware of the nuances of spiritual illness as they have experienced it first hand is given the power to be of unique use to those who suffer from this illness as they have found the way out with God's grace.

After the endurance race through those steps we are handed a sort of super cape by our Maker and hold a special place in His army. My appreciation for this "cape" does not spill over from an over-inflated ego or arrogance. It was paid for dearly by not only myself but my wife and children, my family and all those whom I've touched over the years with my own spiritual deficiency. Hence that sense that my amends will last the rest of my life through a demonstration powered by humility. I have found that the spirit of continued work with others, not just alcoholics, is not to create a fallible dependency on myself or another meatsuit but to guide them home to their own Maker. And this has been my effort powered by Him since he had mercy on my spirit when I offered that first earnest prayer out of that combat-roll on that dark morning. I was allowed to witness a few of these experiences of men willing to try something different and the most powerful one was a dear friend Frank who is no longer with us.

I watched Frank gain his own freedom from that darkness of spiritual illness and then was allowed to watch him gain that freedom from his body as his spirit made its way home to God.

45 - THERE IS MORE TO YOU THAN YOUR MEATSUIT

I met Frank many years before we would work together through this set of principles. We would get to know one another over the years through the men's groups that I administered. The groups where we tried collectively to practice these very principles yet always seemed to fall short of their intent. If I told you he was a bit crazy that would be a serious understatement. He was downright nasty and angry. The difference between his temperament and mine was that he was expressive with it. He wore it on his sleeve and seemed to have a pride about it. He didn't care who saw it and knew it whereas I tried with all of my effort to disguise it, and hide.

Much like our spirits can see and recognize each other through the eyes, and heart, and even our auras, the madness within me could relate to the madness within Frank. We were kindred in spirit, a sick and maladjusted spirit that is. My own spiritual deficiency could easily honor and attract the same in others like a magnet to steel. It was that water seeks its own level quality. Yet there was a fear I felt when near him.

He was so explosive and expressive that I was always at the ready for him to do something crazy. He spoke about blowing things up and other things he wished to do, so much so that I thought about frisking him when he arrived at the meeting each week and told him so. The other men grew visibly uncomfortable when he would go off on another tirade about this and that and they and those as he viciously pointed that finger in contempt.

He was angry and loaded with resentments. We would come to enjoy many conversations as we tried to figure this mess of resentment out.

Over the years his spirit did calm down as did mine. We made incremental progress, individually and together, yet always seemed to fall short of that freedom from the destructive power a resentment has. We always fell short of gaining a *mastery* over the resentments. That full understanding of what God's will is for us and freedom from judgment and criticism and that position of knowing our own place, and purpose, within God's universe.

Frank was one of the men I would approach after I had my spiritual awakening and we would learn so much from one another. I would be a guide that would bring him the good news that I had found.

After my own experience I walked away from those men's groups as I became aware of their weakness, there lack of real directions. I took this new experience and set of pointed directions and formed a new group of men, most of which had been a part of those other groups over the years.

We met one night a week in the back of my

flower shop and went through the experience of those pioneers and began to follow their directions that are weaved within. Frank was a part of this as well. The design room in the back of the shop bulged at the seams with better than twenty-five men and you could feel the camaraderie between us all.

As we approached the moral inventory I handed each man a blank notebook and a pen fearing that many of them would appear the following week with the excuse that they didn't have a chance to get one themselves. I simply gave them the first part of the writing instructions, a timeline of sorts, a relatively easy task. The following week they showed up and a handful of the men had it finished. I invited all of them back the next week after I gave them the next part of the writing and asked those who hadn't completed the first part to do so. Many of the men did not return the following week and explained the reason for not doing so with a wide range of excuses. Many excuses that I would come to hear over and over and over as I worked with others. They were *excuses* and I would come to know the actual *reason*. The fact of the matter is that many will not do the heavy lifting because they do not have a desperation about them that calls forth a willingness to be free. And perhaps the delusion that they are somehow winning at the game of life is there as well. As my own God-consciousness and understanding of this illness grew over time I would watch these men helplessly. As helpless as the woman who could only watch her husband that I spoke to in the last chapter. And it became confusing and discomfiting.

Frank was the only man out of these better than twenty-five to keep moving forward and we would continue along together, one on one, to get him free of resentment and fear and back to his Maker.

Frank trudged through the process and kept trudging the path. His amazement at what he discovered equaled my own and he was a joy to watch as his own spirit began to awaken and be reconnected to God. It was like looking in the mirror at my own experience. As unpleasant as the process was for him he could *feel* it as he went through. He saw the value of what those pioneers found and achieved, as did I.

He was able to break free of that bondage of self and was able to shed his past. He was able to make the approach to those he had harmed and understood that his amends would last a lifetime. He also understood that if he wished to keep what he had found he would have to search for those who wished to be free and were willing to do that heavy lifting.

Frank came to a place of acceptance, an acceptance of what God's plan was for him and when he was diagnosed with cancer we grew even closer. We had grown close years before by that attraction through illness and madness, our common problem, yet now we were joined together through God, our common solution to the spiritual malady.

We would speak often as he went through treatment and he often wondered if his cancer was related to all of that anger and resentment he had held throughout his years as it is just as insidious and confusing.

As he was nearing the end I was called to the house he was staying at. It would be one of the last times that I would see him alive. When I arrived he was laying in bed, resting. I entered the room and I sensed a peace within, within the room and within Frank.

I laid beside him in the bed as we faced one another and locked eyes. I took his hand and asked him a few questions. One of which was a question that I asked him months before as he finished up his confession that I had the honor of hearing.

"Frank." I asked as he tried to close his eyes and drift away.

"Yes?" As he slowly opened them and lock his gaze on my face with a faint smile.

"Is there anything you wish to discuss or leave here in words before you pass and go home to your Maker?"

"We already covered everything." He whispered to me.

We just laid there and I watched him close those eyes that were filled with such fire and venom years before yet were now relaxed. Some time went by; we just laid there. Every once and a while he opened his eyes and would look at me. He would smile and that smile was the most peaceful version and indication of where his spirit was, and landed, before he left.

"Frank."

He opened those eyes, those windows to his soul.

"Can I ask you another question?"

"Yes Bobby."

"Are you good with your Maker?"

He didn't answer this right away, there was a pause.

A tear left his eye and made its way down his temple. I let go of his hand to wipe it away.

"I am." He closed his eyes again with a renewed

smile.

We laid together for a while and held hands.

"I love you Frank."

"I love you too...thank you."

These were some of the last words I would hear from Frank and he passed away a short while later leaving behind more than he could ever imagine to me, and to many others. Including all of the others I would work with and will work with.

Where once our madness invited each of us to unite we were able to unite in God's grace and mercy. We were two wretches that were saved, ultimately able to be of service to God in saving other wretches. It is magical. I was honored and humbled when his family asked me to do a reading at his service after he passed away.

This is the purpose that I believe God has brought me to, today. The ability to recognize that I'm not simply a meatsuit running around the planet put here only to fulfill my own selfish wants and needs. Today I believe we are all spirits living a spiritual existence yet are allowed to have a human experience as well. We are allowed to exercise our freewills like none of God's other creations and I would be foolish to think that there would be any success in this without Him after the divinely inspired life that I've lived. All of it, the good, the bad and the ugly.

46 - A GROWING PURPOSE

Frank was given a service in the parish I practice being a holiday catholic at of which I became very close to the priest who ministered there. There was something inside of me that would have loved to have spoken a few words about what Frank had found while here. God. I would have to settle for my thoughts of him and my renewed spirit to carry this message.

As we sat in the church for the service and followed that typical outline of a few readings and what not, the priest rose and went to the lectern where he spoke on the family's behalf and shared what they had told him about Frank. From Father Ron came exactly what I wished to speak about as this is what his family had relayed to him.

He spoke to Frank's decision of turning his own life and will over to God's care and what he had found as a result of it. I fell into tears and had this feeling creep up on me. My mind wandered to what it would be like when I'm allowed to leave here. The hereafter.

For many years I attempted to evade God, and as

my catalog of harms I had done to others built and grew mountainous, I began to fear the hereafter. It wasn't that "Your soul is going to hell and you will burn forever" fear. It was a fear of possibly meeting my Maker and being held accountable for that crazy-ass self will. Or even spending eternity in purgatory as a lost and listless soul.

One of the greatest parts of being freed from that spiritual malady is that with time and practice and the maintenance of relying and trusting on God the fears fall away. This was my experience, I became fearless in all areas of my life, especially the hereafter. Ironically as I grasped this new life and was becoming more God-conscious I desired more in the way of a life and more in the way of awareness of Him. It was that nourishing to me. It created that much relief, far more relief than the alcohol and drugs created when I first started with them.

As I journeyed on and tried to fit myself to be of maximum service to God and to my fellows the feelings and thoughts of wanting to go home to God became more frequent. As I grew more aware not only of Him but of the spiritual sickness I could now clearly see in individuals, groups of individuals, and even entire countries, there came this longing to be free from here. Like if I had my way and could fully dictate my life experience I would have cut it short, returning to God in spirit, leaving my body behind. As I was new to this way of life I couldn't fully define my thoughts or feelings yet they would be defined by the life experience of others. At times I gain more understanding of His will for me by watching others than I do by watching myself. Watching the failures and successes, the unconsciousness and awareness, the defeats and triumphs.

As the old skin on my meatsuit was shed and a new one began growing I was be surrounded by men and women who would teach me with their words and through their own examples many things that I neglected to notice growing up and many things I would need to know as I journeyed if I was to have any success at remaining awake. Some of these teachers were downright brutal when teaching, as I have been at times, and still others were as gentle as a fluffy cloud looks, as I have been at times.

One of these men came into my life and his presence created many shifts over a period of two years as we got closer. He too would eventually pass away from cancer. While he went about his treatments and really couldn't be around too many people as he didn't want to catch an infection we began our Sunday night meetings in his home discussing these very principles that allowed us to be reborn.

Many of us who were there had gone through the process and endeavor to live these principles vigilantly. One of these men fell off and as of this writing has yet to find his way back to the path. Still one other came, and to this day as well, can't or won't do the work to get free from the ego and pride. One of these men is now waging his own battle against cancer. (We can put a man on the moon and time it nearly to the second yet can't cure cancer? Maybe it is tied to spiritual disease at some levels.)

Al was the one who cleared up some of the confusion when it came to steps two and three of those twelve steps, two of which are not in that set of six that the pioneers followed before they were expanded. The second step speaks to coming to that place where you understand that God's Power was what restored you to sanity and step three speaks to deciding to turn your life and will over to the care of God. The two steps I've seen many get stuck on, or that created some form of resistance from moving on to the necessary *action*, the work, of the program that ignites the rocket to a spiritual experience.

Al shared and simply stated that if you wished to know what those two steps were about do the work of the rest of the steps and then you will come to know what they mean. You will come to know their meaning by your participation, your effort.

Al displayed a resilience and strength as he journeyed home to God with only brief moments of fear or self-pity. He lived the end of his time here by and with God's grace. He also felt that whatever demonstration and testimony he had offered up until the end would have to suffice for his own amends. I admired this man so much and his readiness to meet his Maker. I admired his loss of fear when it came to the hereafter. And on some levels he defined that feeling I had of wanting to go home to God. Where I once wanted to go home to Him to escape reality Al defined that part of me that wished to go home to quench that thirst we can get when exposed to God's Love and Mercy. That is how real this transformation of spirit can be if you seek it with willingness and a commitment to go deep within instead of keeping it topical or shallow. There were moments while watching him at the end of his life that I would become envious that he was able to go Home.

Al passed away on a Sunday morning nearly a

year ago, as of this writing. I woke early that morning and something told me to get to the hospital. I stopped along the way for a couple of boxes of donuts for the family and when at this iconic donut place I ran into the man who is now battling his own cancer again and told him I was going to the hospital, that I had a feeling Al was going to pass. He followed me down to the hospital and when we arrived Al was indeed near the end.

I've held two men as their spirits have left this three-dimensional world we live in. The first was Papa in the early morning hours years ago before I began that ten years of living without a conscience. Al was the second. Even though both were equally painful there was a profound difference between the two. When Papa passed away I still hadn't enjoyed a shift of consciousness, a spiritual awakening, yet when Al passed away I had already experienced that and was able to be there for his family in a way that I couldn't be for my own so many years before. There is something ethereal about it when you have the ability to think of others more often than yourself. A quality that those pioneers came to understand as well when they spoke to their lives depending on the constant thought of others and how we might be able to meet *their* needs rather than our own selfish needs.

For one to move from that self-absorption to living on the plane of thought with that added layer, that fourth dimension, is a priceless gift. This is what Al taught me the most through his own demonstration while here. Even at his darkest and lowest moments of pain, and worry for his family, he always sought to find out what was going on with others while in conversation with them.

That is an unmerited gift that comes with a spiritual awakening.

47 - A NEW HOPE

We are coming to the end of our journey together, for now. Of course I could ramble on with a continuous testimony of how my perception has been changed by citing more examples but that might distract you from seeing your own as you journey. They are there and they are real. I just couldn't see them because my lenses were all scratched and my vision was hazy. Today my vision is clearer than ever and something deep inside tells me it will become clearer and clearer as time passes and I'm allowed to continue my work with others as God dictates.

One of the most amazing gifts along this plane of recovery and living a spiritual life, instead of just theorizing about it, is the fact that my wife decided to come on this journey with me. Where once she thought the effort of trying to help others get sober was useless she now sees the value in the work I do. Where she once had a faith and believed in God she was able to witness a miracle of His Power in her own husband thereby increasing and deepening her own faith in Him. This became a snowball that grows in size as we share with one another the discoveries made about that mystery. Recovery works much like spiritual illness does, it's infectious.

We are learning to live our lives as spirits, not just humans wrestling our way through life, and every moment spent in this effort has revealed to us that the here and now is not only about being present, it is a present. A gift.

Where I was once, for a great many years, without the power to effect any changes in my life, including those of my thoughts and flaws in my character, I am now empowered to exercise the gift that God allows each of us, a choice, along lines that follow His grace. A change of heart sets a new course and I never had the ability to change my heart yet now I enjoy it. I now believe God hands each of us that freewill to make choices. We have a freedom to choose. Some of us will choose wisely and some of us won't. I now know it's never too late to change our course if we are willing enough to do it. Maybe even desperate enough too.

My hope for you is that *if* you are feeling disconnected and out of sorts you are able to reset your own course. What I've found is that even if God does have a master plan for each of us and if our lives are predetermined perhaps there is a caveat in that plan that allows us to change our course at any time we feel the pull to do that. Maybe, just maybe, this is why He shot us down here with that freewill and a brain to use.

Is my life perfection? Or my spiritual life perfection? No. And yes! I believe it is divinely designed.

I've given you my *testimony* and do hope you haven't found this in poor taste with some of the things I've revealed. If by chance you were moved I applaud this. If you weren't I applaud this as well as I am in no position to place judgment on anyone. If you were inspired to take some steps to adjust the rudders that steer your own guiding forces then my account has been worth the effort. If you come to a decision to explore a new way of living and seek this Power that made all of this possible for me I'm confident this pleases Him. Or Her.

I would offer you my prayers but petitioning God to change you would in essence be telling God what to do and I've found this does not work. I can, always do, and will continue to, think of you, each of you, with the hope that you get to experience freedom from that bondage of self. An experience that frees you from everything that blocks you from what I've come to know is a loving God.

My love goes out to each and every one of you! We are all spirits wrapped in our meatsuits and we are all headed in the same direction and will certainly have different experiences but in the end I believe we will all come to the same place. And that is in the palm of God's hand. It is rare that I speak in absolutes but it's that last piece that I hand to you in this manner.

My love and thoughts to you all.

And

May you recognize that God has indeed blessed you.

EPILOGUE

I may never have the benefit of knowing how God will use this to His advantage or what benefit it has brought to you, if any, but I wish to express my deepest gratitude for coming along on this journey with me. If the countless hours, tears shed, and laughter I experienced as I typed and edited have brought just one glimmer of hope or shift in just one person's perception then my effort was not wasted. We may at times feel as though we have only the effect of a small ripple in that lake of life yet even that one tiny ripple resonates in outward directions. Change is created in the constitution of others by each of us.

There were many times I sat in my dining room or at my design space and typed obsessively with a drive that is not normally my own. There were many times I would review the typing from the previous day as I edited along the way and was amazed at what landed on the paper. Many times I couldn't recall writing what was there. There were times when my wife would say I'm learning things about you I've never known as she reviewed my rough edits. I experienced two blocks as I was writing and signs were sent along the way to guide me.

At times I would sit before my laptop and just watch my fingers move without thought, which was sort of freaky. That Push, "Write," to get all of this down somewhere was evident throughout the entire process and to say I'm pleased that this body of work was completed falls short of the emotion felt. Much like the words I used to describe the spiritual experience I had will always be pale in comparison to the emotion it was wrapped in. In fact the completion of the writing touched off another blast of that bliss felt within that I know is of my Maker.

As I walk away from this title I would be remiss if I didn't extend a thank you to all of those musical artists that seemed to fuel and boost me as I typed. At times I simply had to turn the volume up and watch it happen. And at other times I had to reach into that musical vault from different time periods of my life in an effort to set the steering and direction, and the recall of memories.

There is no doubt that much was left out of the body of work you just read and experienced. A lot of which I would have liked to have included yet felt the *pull* to save it for another time. Of course there were things I wished to share and even though I did receive the consent of others to do so there was also a pull to save this as well.

As this book will certainly resonate with those in recovery and perhaps those who work in the field of recovery the next title will be entirely devoted to recovery as my own experience has come to match those who pioneered this process of recovery decades ago. The pieces that were withheld will more than likely show up there. And if by chance you find yourself with some questions left unanswered they may be addressed in this title. If you wish to ask a question or want deeper detail about my experience embrace the wonder of the web and social media. You may reach me through my website at www.RobertErnestBach.com, or through my Facebook page @Bach.Ernest.Robert.

In the preface I spoke to the fact that there were perhaps two or three books in this mind of mine and that a visit from a friend cleared this up for me. There are indeed two more in there and they were further shaped as I went deeper and deeper into this writing. The greatest part of this is that I now have a choice in what to put forth next.

The first title features a cat that my family and I had. A title I began two years ago, have recently reviewed, and expect to complete by the fall of 2018. His name is Bores and he likes to think he is a "Panther," though he is simply a domestic cat. He is sent here by God on a journey to set a man on a new course. A course he knows only too well as he had the same experience in his last lifetime here as a human. His last lifetime here was as a recovered alcoholic who happened to be one of those pioneers I spoke about throughout this title as well as one of the men who came upon the interpretation of the twelve steps that I happened to apply to my spiritual illness with success. It is a work of fiction yet is wrapped tightly in the real experiences of two men and naturally the fantasy of an overconfident and rather cocky cat who fancies himself a superhero.

The other title will also be along the lines of recovery and will look squarely at the difference between six and twelve steps.

As we reached the end of this title I spoke to a meditation that was shared with me. As a recovered alcoholic it is imperative that I do not rest, or stand still, in my seeking of God. As the problem with the alcoholic certainly does center in his mind it will always be in my best interest to remain sharp in the practicing of these principles. One of the greatest elements is to exercise the ability to just *watch*. Watch for resentment and fear as they crop up. The meditation that I am providing the links for not only saved my life and my sanity but is the most effective tool in detaching from my thoughts. The links are as follows:

Pre-Meditation Talk
www.bit.ly/rmedpep

"Real Meditation for Real Alcoholics"
www.bit.ly/realdaily

I thank you with all that I have for taking this journey with me! I wish you peace and harmony, and maybe just enough pain to create a change within your own life, for you, and for others. And especially for The Grand Architect.

BIBLIOGRAPHY

3
Paley, W. 1851: Evidences of Christianity
London: W. Crowes and Sons

All Others
Wilson, B et al. 1939: Alcoholics Anonymous
New York City: Works Publishing Company

ABOUT THE AUTHOR

Robert is a happily married, father of three residing in coastal Rhode Island. Getting clean and sober at the age of eighteen Robert has endured, and enjoyed, over thirty years of recovery from alcohol and drugs and lives a life second to none as a recovered alcoholic. As an artist he enjoys painting and all things creative in his daily work as a floral designer and wedding planner.

Thank you for taking this journey with me!
Kindly review your experience with my book on Amazon.com

Made in the USA
Columbia, SC
03 August 2017